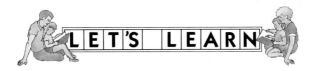

AROUND THE WORLD

Mitchell Beazley

AROUND THE WORLD

CONTENTS

EXPLORING OUR WORLD

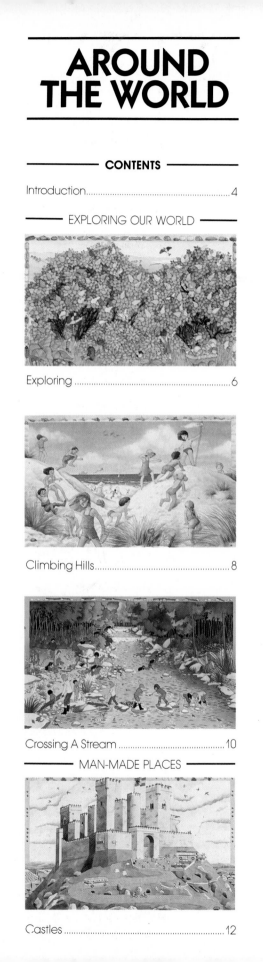

MAN-MADE PLACES

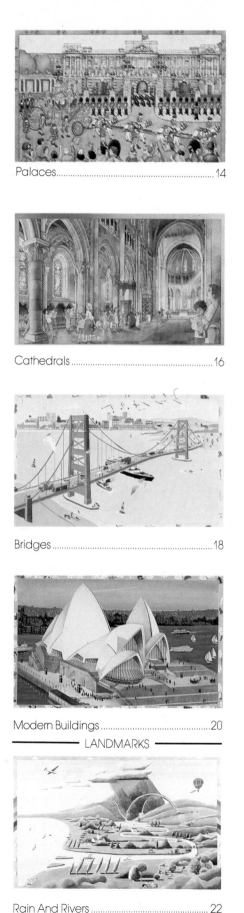

LANDMARKS

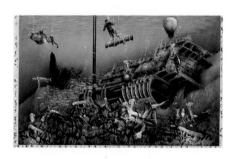

CELEBRATIONS

THE ARTISTS

LET'S LEARN

LANGUAGE AND EDUCATION CONSULTANT

Professor Peter Herriot
Birkbeck College, University of London

LEARNING SKILLS ADVISER

Dr. Sara Meadows
Department of Education
University of Bristol

PLAY AND LEARN ADVISER

Peter Dixon
King Alfred's College, Winchester

ADVISORY PANEL

Gill Barnet
Maxilla Day Nursery Centre, London

Lesley Chandler
Edmund Waller Infants' School, London

Jan Cooper
Centre for Urban Education Studies
Inner London Education Authority

Marion Dowling
Infant and Pre-School Education Adviser
Dorset Education Authority

Joyce Jurica
Centre for Language in Primary Education
Inner London Education Authority

Janet O'Connel
Inner London Pre-School Playgroups Association

Pam Smith
Department of Psychology, Hatfield Polytechnic

John Stannard
Primary Education Adviser
Inner London Education Authority

Joanna Studdert
Centre for Urban Education Studies
Inner London Education Authority

© Mitchell Beazley Publishers 1982
First published 1982
Edited and designed by
Mitchell Beazley Publishers
Mill House 87–89 Shaftesbury Avenue
London W1V 7AD
All rights reserved

ISBN 0 85533 426 6

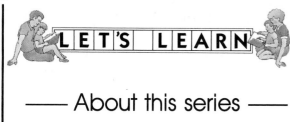

LET'S LEARN

About this series

Young children learning

Children start exploring their world before they can even speak and long before they reach school. You can see their understanding develop by watching the things they do and, as they begin to learn to talk, you can actually hear it because they do much of their thinking aloud either by talking to themselves, or by questioning adults and other children.

Children and adults

During these early years, children do not separate their day into times for learning and times for playing; they learn all the time as they play. This means that the adults who spend most time during the day with a child can enormously assist that child's learning if they treat answering and posing questions as fun, if they go at the child's pace and, perhaps above all, if they spend time talking and doing things together.

Learning by talking

The *Let's Learn* books are planned not only to give you the pleasure that all families get from sharing good books but also to present a wide range of information in specially designed pictures that will encourage your child to talk about them and so come to understand them fully. Time and again you will find your child looking at a picture of a scene he recognizes and seeing far more in it as he talks with you. As he does so, you will notice that your child is gradually acquiring a wider vocabulary and learning to speak more fluently. This, rather than early mastery of mechanical skills, is the vital key to your child's development in the early years. Children who talk fluently master other intellectual skills more easily.

Children gaining skills

The *Let's Learn* books offer a balanced range of early learning skills which will develop all sides of your child's thinking. By practising these skills in ways that will be easy and enjoyable for both of you, you will give your child the start he needs into activities such as reading, calculating, problem solving and logical reasoning, and therefore provide him with a firm foundation which teachers, and others, can build on as he grows older.

Asking questions

The best way to answer a child's question is often to ask another one. By doing so, you can help your child to sort out what he already knows and help him to use that information to begin to answer his own question. If your child seems interested in an idea but can't answer your question, think about how you have asked it. Does he clearly understand what you mean? It's not always easy to rephrase a question so that you are asking the same thing in a simpler way, but you can sometimes make a game of trying to do so. Asking questions that children can't answer is not a clever way to stretch their thinking, but a sure way to confuse them; so, if they really don't know the answer, tell them.

Age range

The *Let's Learn* books are designed for use with children between the ages of three and six. At three your child will already be passing from the simple identification of objects in a picture that many two-year-olds can manage – eg "there's a boat" – and will be ready to work out exactly what is happening in quite complicated pictures. By the time he is six, your child will be quite capable of understanding most of the more advanced ideas that lie behind some of the pictures as well as spotting all the more intricate details.

Terminology

Throughout the text, "younger" and "older" have been used to indicate either end of the three to six range. However, all young children vary enormously in what they can do and how they think and it is impossible to be precise about which child will be able to manage any particular task. Because you will be doing most of this work with one child, children have usually been referred to in the singular and "he" and "she" have been used equally. All the exercises and suggestions are appropriate for children of either sex.

Pace

Children will vary enormously in how much time they want to spend on any one picture, in how often they want to look at it again and in how much more they find to talk about on their second and third looks. It is important not to go too fast. Give your child plenty of time to think round an idea, question you and come up with his own suggestions. Try to stop working on a picture before your child (or you) is bored by it. When you come back to it later, you will find that your child wants to spend longer on it and understands the ideas behind it more fully.

8 Around The World
EXPLORING OUR WORLD
Climbing Hills

Children's answers to the question "Why do we climb hills?" are much the same as the answers an adult mountaineer will give you – because they're there; they're fun; they're a challenge. This picture introduces themes that come up again later in the volume (see p. 28).
□ Climbing can be hard work. You often need to use your arms as well as your legs to help push you up the hill.
□ Once you have climbed to the top you can see how quickly you can get to the bottom of the hill again.
□ Going down is quicker and easier than climbing up.
□ Sand dunes make good places for early climbing adventures. We all do things like climbing or jumping for the first time when we are ready to. Children should not force others to climb or jump when they don't feel confident.

Picture points
1 That girl has already reached the top of the sand hill. She is holding a flag to show that she is "king of the castle".

2 There are different ways of climbing. Look at the girl who is not managing very well. She is not using her arms to help her. Some children find it easier to climb up on their hands and knees. That boy is climbing up the other side, so we can only see his head.

3 It's much slower climbing up the hill than it is sliding down, especially on sand because your feet sink into it.

4 If you are brave you can jump from the top of this hill. The sand is nice and soft to land on.

5 That boy doesn't want to join in the game. He prefers watching the ships out at sea. Why did he climb the hill?

Using The Pictures

The text is organized in a logical order that follows the way most children will approach a picture. They are likely to want to scan it and work out what is going on, then come to talk more generally about it and then be interested in the associated learning skills. However, your child may prefer to start with one of the activities in the back of the book and you should usually let him start where he wants to.

Main Ideas

1 The italic type tells you why the picture is included in the volume while the points immediately below outline the main ideas behind it. Most of these ideas will seem startlingly obvious, but children need to think gradually about things that adults often take for granted. When you first look at a picture together, let your child talk about it in his own words for as long as he wants to. (This may only be for a few minutes with younger children.) Try to follow up the comments that seem likely to lead to further talking. The main text is written in a style that young children can follow if you simply read it to them; it is even better if you can adapt the text and have an entirely natural chat.

Picture Points

2 Check through the picture points and talk about any parts of the picture that have not already been mentioned. This may give you the chance to help your child to identify new objects or introduce new ideas. There are suggested answers (in brackets) to many of the questions to show what you can reasonably expect from your child, but remember that a child's logic may produce all sorts of ideas and it is always worth finding out the thinking behind an apparently illogical answer.

Talking Points

3 The talking points provide appropriate conversation topics; try to have a good conversation rather than accepting, or giving, one-word answers. You will need to listen as well as talk, ask as well as answer questions, make jokes and, at all stages, remind your child of experiences you have already shared which relate to the ideas in the picture. When children are really interested in a subject, they are likely to go on asking questions about it at times when you are not expecting them. Although it is not always easy to be alert to this, do try to respond with a positive answer that shows you know what they are thinking about and that you are interested in their ideas.

Learning Skills

4 Practise the Learning Skills whenever your child is interested. There are two different skills on each page: the first one is usually easier than the second. The italic type at the head of each section advises you on the purpose of each exercise and the questions in each section usually go from easier to harder. Ask the questions your child can answer, come back to the more difficult ones on another occasion. The skills on each page are the ones that are most appropriate for that picture and the books have been planned so that all skills are practised at different levels. Once you are used to introducing learning skills, you will find that you can practise most of them with any of the pictures. When you first look at the suggestions for learning skills you may think that your child has already mastered them; for instance, that he knows what all the colours are. You will soon realize, however, that children can have a certain amount of knowledge without a great deal of understanding. Enjoyable practice that goes carefully over each step is the way to increase his understanding and make him feel confident about learning.

AROUND THE WORLD
About This Book

Widening horizons

It is not easy to give young children a sense of the world beyond their own immediate home environment. On the other hand, it is not, as some people suggest, impossible. Children can perfectly well understand that there are other people and places in the world. You don't need to tell them, for instance, how far away, or even where, China is; that's the sort of information they can't hope to understand properly. In fact, they won't try to understand this kind of information because they will quite happily accept that China is out there waiting to be explored, that its people are interesting and that their customs are different from our own, but no more peculiar.

Children exploring the world

This book emphasizes the point that people all over the world undertake very similar activities even though they may take quite different approaches to them. It also gives children some sense of the immense excitement exploration can give, whether it is simply going on holiday to a new place or penetrating the deepest jungle. Your children's first explorations just beyond home can give you some worrying moments. It is quite important not to restrict their adventures, but you do need to give them some firm rules and also make clear that there are some places where they must never go without you, for instance, ponds, main roads and caves.

Television and children

Long before children actually visit many of the world's famous buildings and physical features, they see television programmes about them. Very often these appear as the background to a story or news item and the programme may pass on before children can begin to think carefully about what they are seeing. Young children need a chance to "stop the film" so that they can explore all aspects of a scene that has interested them and a picture can help them to do that. The pictures in this book give a representative selection of buildings and physical features and the text shows different ways to talk about unfamiliar but exciting sights. It should be easy to adapt the suggestions made here to fit any places that particularly interest you and your family.

Main Themes

In addition to giving information and ideas, this book is organized in four sections which follow a developing theme. Younger children will be too busy coming to grips with all kinds of information to notice this but you may find that older children are ready to start thinking in broader terms.

Exploring Our World

Children start exploring at an early age and should be encouraged to do so safely in numbers rather than alone, and as near to home as possible. They should be taught a number of firm safety rules before they set out.

Man-made Places

People have created beautiful buildings and structures in all parts of the world. Many of the most famous ones are many centuries old, but a few are modern. People visit these buildings for different reasons.

Landmarks

Many of the world's physical features are famous because they are immensely attractive. Exploring them can present irresistible challenges. Children will only come to appreciate how enormously varied the Earth's surface is as they see pictures or films and as they gradually begin to visit a variety of different places.

Celebrations

All over the world people celebrate similar occasions in a variety of different ways. These celebrations have often survived from times when they had more meaning and importance than they do today but they still provide good reasons for relaxing and enjoyable festivities.

Key Ideas

- ☐ Children begin exploring at very early ages and it usually becomes a lifetime's occupation.

- ☐ There are interesting places wherever you go and it is always worth stopping to visit them.

- ☐ Some famous places are man-made, others are natural.

- ☐ All people have celebrations, but they often celebrate in different ways.

- ☐ Celebrations are enjoyed by people of all ages, including children.

EXPLORING OUR WORLD

Exploring

Anything to do with discovering and exploring is fascinating to children, especially if they can find a place which is new ground, but safe enough for them to explore by themselves.

☐ New discoveries, such as a bush, shed or cupboard, have the attraction of being a private and comfortable place as well as being strange and possibly slightly frightening.

☐ Bushes give shelter and can be dry in the middle. They make perfect places for exploring activities.

☐ Children explore by looking at a new place carefully and slowly, and often return to it several times.

☐ Many places that children explore are already the homes of birds and insects. All creatures – and their homes – should be respected.

Picture points

1 These lucky children have found a lovely place to explore. How many children are there?

2 Some of the bush is low on the ground, other parts are high in the air. Who is exploring the highest part? Who, the lowest? Who, the darkest?

3 Two children have found interesting insects. What are the insects? (Caterpillar, beetle.)

4 One boy is near a nest. Why must he be very careful? (Scaring birds, damaging nest and eggs.)

5 You can see some of the creatures that live in or near the bush. Let's look in the border at what they are.

6 The explorers have brought a pram with them. How will they use the things in the pram?

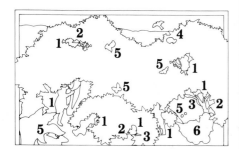

Talking Points

1 Do you know any good hiding places like this bush? Where are they?

2 Why do you have to be careful when you explore? (Breaking branches, sharp objects, getting lost.)

3 What would the bush be like in the winter? Would it still have flowers and leaves on it?

4 Something will happen to the eggs and the caterpillar – what? (Eggs hatch, caterpillar becomes butterfly.)

Learning Skills

How would you feel if . . . ?
Any adult will know immediately what the inside of this bush must be like; but children find it harder to look at a picture this way. They can't describe what they can't see. Remind them of their own adventures to help them do so.
☐ These children are exploring the bushes. Have you ever done that? I wonder what it's like in there. Is it a bit dark? Is it wet, or dry and dusty?
☐ Would you like to explore a big bush? Would it be fun or frightening – or both? The dark might be rather nasty and sharp branches might scratch you, but they wouldn't be too bad, would they? And think what interesting things you might find there.

Numbers
You need to begin early number work carefully. Take it slowly and try to make it fun by concentrating on things that are bound to interest children. Stop if they are clearly not interested.
☐ Do you know what a pair is? It means that there are two of something. You've got one pair of arms. That means you've got two arms altogether. I'm wondering how many pairs of legs there are in the picture.
☐ How many pairs of legs have you got? And so how many legs altogether?
☐ Do you know how many pairs of legs a hedgehog has (two) and a butterfly (three) and a beetle (three) and a bee (three) and a bird?
☐ Now let's put down a block for every pair of legs we can see in the picture. How many blocks have we got? So how many legs altogether? (Tell them if they don't know.)
Story and games on p.50

EXPLORING OUR WORLD

Climbing Hills

Children's answers to the question "Why do we climb hills?" are much the same as the answers an adult mountaineer will give you – because they're there; they're fun; they're a challenge. This picture introduces themes that come up again later in the volume (see p. 28).

☐ Climbing can be hard work. You often need to use your arms as well as your legs to help push you up the hill.

☐ Once you have climbed to the top you can see how quickly you can get to the bottom of the hill again.

☐ Going down is quicker and easier than climbing up.

☐ Sand dunes make good places for early climbing adventures. We all do things like climbing or jumping for the first time when we are ready to. Children should not force others to climb or jump when they don't feel confident.

Picture points

1 That girl has already reached the top of the sand hill. She is holding a flag to show that she is "king of the castle".

2 There are different ways of climbing. Look at the girl who is not managing very well. She is not using her arms to help her. Some children find it easier to climb up on their hands and knees. That boy is climbing up the other side, so we can only see his head.

3 It's much slower climbing up the hill than it is sliding down, especially on sand because your feet sink into it.

4 If you are brave you can jump from the top of this hill. The sand is nice and soft to land on.

5 That boy doesn't want to join in the game. He prefers watching the ships out at sea. Why did he climb the hill?

Talking Points

1 We can climb on different things. You climb on the climbing frame in the park. What other things can people climb? (Stairs, ladders, trees, etc.)

2 What makes it hard to climb a hill? (How steep it is, how slippery it is.)

3 Do you think the other children mind being pushed down by the "king of the castle"? Would you mind? Can you explain how to play? Do you know the words that the king calls out?

Learning Skills

Sand play
Sand, like water, is magic to children. Nobody would want to spoil the pure fun they have with it, but as they get older you can help them to think constructively about the things they have already found out in play.

☐ (Pour dry sand into the top half of an old detergent bottle.) Look, it trickles through the nozzle. Let's see what patterns we can make by pouring sand on the ground.

☐ Could you run upstairs and back before all the sand empties out? (Older children may time other activities in "bottles of sand".)

☐ What happens if we pour some water on to sand? (It sticks together.) Then what can we do with it? Could you make sandcastles with dry sand?

☐ Sand pours when it's dry and sticks together when it's wet, so what is it made of? (Lots and lots of tiny bits. Older children may be able to tell you a lot more about those bits by using a magnifying glass.)

What people are doing
Talk about all the different actions that are shown in the picture. Use a variety of action words while you are doing this.

☐ That's a steep hill made of sand. Show me the people who are climbing up. Which are using their hands to climb as well as their feet? Why? Can you think of a word which describes that way of climbing? (Scrambling.) Who's going faster, the scramblers or the girl who's trying to walk up?

☐ Who is sliding down the hill? Who is jumping down the hill? Who is already at the bottom? Who is standing on top of the hill and looking out to sea?

Story and games on p.51

EXPLORING OUR WORLD

Crossing A Stream

Few activities give children more pleasure than playing by water. In damming and trying to cross a stream as seen here, they are exploring one of man's oldest problems while learning about the force and flow of water.

☐ Getting across water without becoming wet is difficult even if the stream is quite narrow and not very deep.

☐ Stepping stones and bridges are two of the simplest ways to cross water.

☐ Streams are rarely still; the water is always moving and getting round or over any obstructions it meets.

☐ Children have to be very careful when playing near water. There should always be adults nearby.

Picture points

1 These families have come for a picnic together by a stream. What time of year is it? (Autumn – colours, falling leaves.)

2 Can the children cross the stream without getting wet? (No, see gap.) What makes streams difficult to cross?

3 What are the children going to use to try to finish off their crossing? Does it look long enough?

4 The girl on the stones is holding her arms out to help her balance. Why is she finding it difficult? (Small stone, wide gap, slippery.)

5 What can you see that can cross the stream without using the stones? (Dog, birds, person on bridge.)

6 Can you see the twigs caught in the stones? How did they get there? (Water carries things along with it.) Which way is the water flowing?

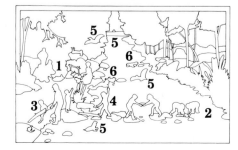

Talking Points

1 How many people could use the stepping stones at one time?

2 Suppose that lots of people want to cross a stream or river at the same place, would stepping stones be the best way? How else can you cross a river? (Bridge, boat, plane, tunnel, swim.)

3 How can you tell how deep the water is? (Dog, boy's boots.) You can't be sure though, water is often deeper than it looks. It may be deeper near the waterfall than by the stones.

4 Suppose there was an accident; who would rush to the rescue? (Grown-ups; don't go near water without one!)

Learning Skills

Where things are
Children don't find it as easy as we may to understand everything about a picture on the first glance. If you concentrate on important words, you can help them to search through the picture.
☐ Who is up above the stream? Who else? (Have they noticed man on bridge?) Anything else? (Birds.)
☐ Who is in the stream? Who else? Who might be in it soon if she is not careful?
☐ Can you see a stone above the stream? What would happen if it was dropped? Who would get wet because they are so near?
☐ What do you think the smallest boy is pointing at? (The birds are American belted kingfishers.)

Water flow
Moving water is an important topic that usually interests children. There are other pictures on this topic in this volume and in LAND, SEA AND SKY.
☐ Can you see the leaves and twigs in the water? Can you see some that are moving along in the water? Why are they moving? (They float. The water moves downhill.)
☐ Can you see some leaves and twigs that are not moving? Why aren't they moving? (Caught behind stones.)
☐ What happens to the water when it comes up against something? Does it just stop? (Goes round or over.)
☐ Could you make the water stop? Would it be fun to try?
Story and games on p.52

MAN-MADE PLACES

Castles

The main purpose of this picture of a castle in Europe is to encourage children to think that castles are exciting places to visit. It also helps them to start to learn why people built them in the past.

☐ Castles attract a great many visitors who come to look round, take photographs and walk round the walls and passages.

☐ Most castles were built a long time ago. They were built to be very strong and many have lasted up to the present day. The thick, tall walls made them very hard to attack.

☐ People lived in the castle all the time. When they were attacked by the enemy, they had enough food inside the castle to live for months.

Picture points

1 It must be a hard climb to get to the very top of that castle. Who has managed to get highest? Who has still got a long way to climb?

2 People don't attack castles today, but some children are having fun pretending to fight with swords and cannons. How many cannonballs does each cannon in the border have?

3 What do you think the men near the coach are pointing at?

4 The workmen repairing the walls will have to be very careful not to drop anything. What are they doing?

5 You can see how tall the walls are. It must have been very hard for attackers to climb up them.

6 Can you see the balloon? Those people have just let go of it. Where do you think it will go? What else can you see blowing in the wind? (The flag.)

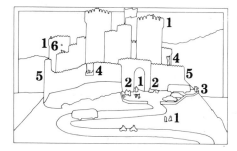

Talking Points

1 Why do you think they built the castle right at the top of the hill? (To make it hard to capture, to have a good view.)

2 A king and queen might have lived in this castle. Who else? (Soldiers, knights, children, servants.)

3 Would you like to live in this castle? Point to the windows of the room you would like to live in.

4 Would you like to visit this castle one day? Would you want to cycle all the way up that hill or would you rather go by coach?

5 What would you most want to look at? Do you think this castle has dungeons/a well/a museum with old weapons in?

Learning Skills

Colours
Work on colours starts with simple naming, but older children can begin to realize that changes in the light can affect the colours they see.
☐ Show me something red. (And so on.)
☐ What colour is the castle? What colours are the cars? What colours are on the hill? (Green grass, yellow rocks, grey road.)
☐ It's nice and sunny and bright outside, but the castle hasn't got many windows. Will it be sunny inside or rather dark? What colour will the stone seem to be when the sun isn't shining on it? (Probably grey.)
☐ What will it be like right up at the top of the castle where those people are? (Sunny and bright again.)

How we see things
It is difficult for children to learn that things look smaller when they are some distance away. You will need to practise this with them.
☐ Look how tall the castle is. Which is the highest part?
☐ Can you see the people up near there? Do they look big or small?
☐ What about the coaches? Do they look big or small? Are they big or small compared with the cars?
☐ If you were on top of the castle, what would the coaches look like? Bigger or smaller than they look now? What would the flag look like?
Story and games on p.53

MAN-MADE PLACES

Palaces

Palaces are usually very large and splendid buildings where kings and queens sometimes live, or used to live.

☐ Buckingham Palace is the London home of Queen Elizabeth II. Her special flag is flown when she is staying there.

☐ Palaces have far more rooms, windows and balconies than ordinary houses and some have large gardens.

☐ A great many people are needed to look after the Palace and to help the Queen with her duties.

☐ Many people want to see the Queen and her famous Palace.

☐ The Queen only wears her crown and ceremonial robes on very special occasions. She sometimes rides in her golden coach on these days.

Picture points

1 A palace is a large, beautiful building with many rooms that often have fine furniture and paintings in them.

2 The Queen needs many people to help her look after her Palace. Some of the workers who live at Buckingham Palace are looking out of the window to watch the procession.

3 All those guardsmen standing to attention are guarding the Palace. Their uniforms show what their job is.

4 Those other men marching beside the Queen's coach look splendid, don't they? Their clothes are just like the ones that people wore a long time ago.

5 The Queen sometimes stands on the decorated balcony to wave to the cheering crowds.

6 Can you see the band? What kind of music do you think they play when the Queen goes out in her coach?

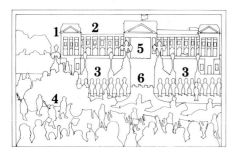

Talking Points

1 What do you have to do to get a good view in a crowd? Who can see best?

2 All the Queen's horses have to be carefully ridden so that the cheering crowds don't frighten them. Would you like to ride one of the grey horses?

3 Can you see a policeman? What does he do in a crowd? When were you last in a crowd where policemen helped you?

Learning Skills

Counting
This exercise moves from basic counting to making comparisons. These may involve counting; using memory to remember the first number while you are counting the second; and then comparing the two totals.
☐ There are lots of things we could count together here, aren't there? How many horses are there? How many coachmen riding them? (Call the one nearest the coach "one". Work forwards.)
☐ Can you see how many people are inside the coach?
☐ How many wheels can you see?
☐ Are there more soldiers or more people in the crowd? Do you think you can see all the crowd?
☐ Are there more little flags or more big ones?
☐ What would be very hard to count because there are so many? (Windows.)

What will happen next?
Children need to practise thinking ahead, especially when one event could end in all sorts of different ways.
☐ The Queen is going somewhere in her coach. Where do you think? (To meet another important person.) What will all these people in the crowd do when she's gone?
☐ There might be another crowd of people at the place she's going to. What will they do when they see her?
☐ What do you think the Queen will do when she meets the other person? (Greet him and take him in the coach.) Where will they go together? (Back to the palace.) What will they do there? (Have a banquet.) (Many children will come up with their own imaginative ideas here. Follow these rather than forcing them to think along your lines or our suggestions.)
Story and games on p.54

MAN-MADE PLACES

Cathedrals

When children visit historical buildings they may well be more interested in what they see happening there now than in the cultural and religious aspects.

☐ A cathedral is a very large church. It was probably built a long time ago by builders who made the building as beautiful as they possibly could.

☐ Tourists visit cathedrals to look at the colourful windows, high ceilings, carved stone and paintings.

☐ Although different religions have different kinds of buildings, many of the ceremonies inside them are similar. They usually involve some form of prayer and worship.

Picture points

1 There are lots of people visiting the cathedral. Can you see anyone looking at the ceiling, or drawing a picture of a stone face, or lighting a candle?

2 The guide is showing these children around. She knows all about the cathedral and tells interesting stories about things that happened there.

3 One person is dressed very differently from everyone else. He is the priest, who leads religious services. Sometimes he goes up the stairs to speak from the pulpit. Can you see where that is?

4 People who have died are sometimes buried in the cathedral. Can you see the statues of them lying down?

5 All the lovely windows are made of coloured glass. When the sun shines through them, it looks as if the sunlight is coloured too. Can you see any coloured sun?

6 There are the workmen on a tall plat-form. What are they doing? (Repairs.)

Talking Points

1 Can you see someone who is more interested in rushing round than in looking at the cathedral? What is her mum looking at? The little girl doesn't want to look at the windows. Do you think her mum should let her wander off or not?

2 The pillars have to be very strong because they hold the cathedral up. What do you think they are made of? (Stone.)

Learning Skills

Shapes

With this picture, you can talk about shapes and how we describe them. We've talked about straight and curved here, but there is also long, thin, round, square, twiddly, etc.

☐ Some parts of the cathedral are very straight (stand stiffly yourself). Can you show them to me?

☐ Some parts are curved and beautifully bent. Can we both stand like that? Can you show me the curved parts?

☐ Do you know the name of the shape we get when two curves join together? It's an arch. Where are the arches?

☐ Where do the arches and the straight bits join together? Do you know why they do? (They hold the roof up.)

Patterns

Carvings nearly always interest children. Talking about them helps children to understand what they can do with different materials themselves.

☐ Can you see all the patterned bits of the cathedral? Show me the curly flower patterns and the faces. What are they made of? (Stone.)

☐ How do you think someone made them? (Children will have all sorts of ideas, not necessarily right ones. Let them explore these notions.)

☐ I think they carved them out of a big block of stone. What sort of tool do you think they used? Would a knife be strong enough to cut stone? Maybe they used a chisel and hammer.

☐ Is there anything else in the cathedral that is carved? (Top of pulpit.) What is that made of? (Wood.)

☐ Have we got anything at home we could carve together? (Try a block of soap, or anything else that is soft enough for children to manage without the danger of sliding knives, etc.)

Story and games on p.55

MAN-MADE PLACES

Bridges

As children begin to appreciate bridges, they also learn important ideas about crossing from one side to another and passing over and under.

☐ Bridges link the two sides of a river and usually carry roads or railways. Wide rivers need long bridges.

☐ There has to be enough space below the bridge for the ships and boats travelling along the river.

☐ Modern bridges are designed to be as graceful as they are useful.

Picture points

1 The cars and lorries on our side of the bridge are crossing it to reach the city. Show me the way they will go. Other cars and lorries are coming away from the city towards us. Where do you think they are going? (Accept any sensible answer, but encourage good guesses.)

2 Look at the big ship going under the bridge. Do you think it's going to get underneath? Is there enough room?

3 There are plenty of smaller boats on the river. They go up and down every day so they pass under the bridge lots of times. Would you like to do that?

4 It's very important to keep the bridge strong and safe. The iron gets very rusty and dangerous if the painters don't paint it often.

5 How many different sorts of motor vehicles are crossing the bridge?

6 Now let's look carefully at the bridge. There are the tall straight supports with the curved wire ropes going over them. They hold the bridge up. (This idea is worth trying, but don't worry if they can't understand. Even older children will find this difficult.)

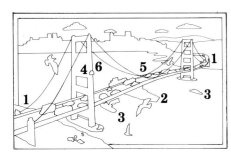

Talking Points

1 How funny that the seagulls seem to be bigger than the boats or the people. Why do you think that is? (Closer.)

2 Show me all the things in the picture and the border that can cross the river without using the bridge. What can they each do that people can't?

3 It must have taken a long time to build that huge bridge. Which bit of the bridge would they start to build first? (The supports.)

4 There are several ways of getting from one side to another. How many can you think of? What about one you can't see here? (Tunnel.) Is crossing the bridge the best way? How is it better? (Follow your child's answer, but question as closely as you can.)

Learning Skills

Position
Practising words that show position helps your child to work out the differences between them and so start to use them properly. Once you are sure the words are understood, try for some jokes and unlikely situations.
☐ Show me all the things above the bridge. (Gull, aeroplane, clouds.)
☐ And what's going over the bridge?
☐ How many things are going under?
☐ Could any of the things going over the bridge go under it? Could a car? Could a bird? Could a plane? (Yes, but it's dangerous.)
☐ What about the boats – could they go over the bridge? (Smaller ones could go over on a trailer.)

What things look like
It's not easy for children to think their way into a picture and understand what someone in it can see.
☐ Imagine you are on a boat just coming towards the city. What could you see first? (The bridge.)
☐ What could you see as you begin to go under the bridge? (Bottom of bridge, bottom of city buildings, etc.)
☐ Then what as you come out the other side? (Whole city stretched out.) What would it all look like at night?
☐ What an exciting place to build a bridge. Everyone sailing to the city sees the bridge first and then the city.
Story and games on p.56

MAN-MADE PLACES

Modern Buildings

Children can learn that there are famous buildings to see in all countries but they are usually quite old. Sydney Opera House in Australia is one of the most famous modern buildings.

☐ This very unusual building is not very old but it is very famous because it is so beautiful and because it was very difficult to build.

☐ Most buildings have straight walls, roofs and windows, but the people who built this one wanted to have curved "flowing" shapes. All sorts of people had to work together to build it.

☐ In Sydney Opera House many concerts, ballets and operas take place.

Picture points

1 Sydney Opera House is built right on the edge of the water so all kinds of ships sail near it. The city buildings rise up behind the ships. The Opera House, ships on the water and buildings together make a wonderful sight.

2 The builders hoped that the roofs would have the same shapes as the billowing yacht sails in the harbour. Do you think they do?

3 There are lots of people arriving at the Opera House. What can they do while they are waiting for the concert to start? (Watch fire-eater and juggler; admire building; lean on rails and look at view.)

4 The people inside will get a splendid view of the harbour and town. What are some of the things they will see when they look out of the big windows?

5 Can you point to the musicians? What sort of musical instruments do you think they've got in their cases?

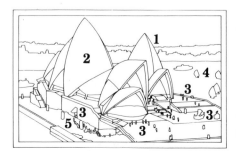

Talking Points

1 Opera singers, musicians and ballet dancers are called entertainers. They do things to interest and amuse us like singing, playing music, dancing (discuss TV personalities). Can you spot some other entertainers in the picture? (Fire-eater.) Can you remember some others? (Circus performers, etc.)

2 We can see people in the picture who have different jobs to do: sing, play, juggle, etc. Can we think of people who we can't actually see but who still have jobs to do with the picture? (Driver of pleasure boat, driver of coach, yachtsman, Opera House window cleaner, etc.)

Learning Skills

How to tell people about your visits
Try to adapt this exercise to suit any visit you have made together recently.
☐ Imagine we went to see this building. How could we tell Granny (or another suitable person) about it?
☐ Could you describe it just in words? (Try, so they see how difficult it is.)
☐ Could you send her a picture of it? How would you do that? (Buy postcard, then write a message on it, put address on it, buy stamp, find post-box.)
☐ The pictures in the border show postcards of famous places round the world. Do you recognize any of them? (Older children may know a few.)

Shapes
When children start to explore shapes and try to build them, they will come up against problems they almost certainly won't be able to solve. It's quite good for them to try to tackle these, as they need to learn what they can't do as well as what they can, but you need to watch to make sure they don't simply get frustrated.
☐ Show me all the straight lines (on side of building, kiosks on promenade, masts, steps, etc).
☐ Now let's look for curves.
☐ What shape are your building blocks? Could you build something the same shape as the kiosks or one of the city buildings in the background?
☐ Could you build something the same shape as the Opera House roof with your blocks? What kind of material would you need? (Try to lead towards something which pours and sets, but your child may well not get there.)
Story and games on p.57

LANDMARKS

Rain And Rivers

This picture helps children to talk in general terms about the weather and about what rivers are. They can find out about specific weather conditions in LAND, SEA AND SKY, *pp. 6–15.*

☐ Rain falls from dark clouds which often blot out the sun.

☐ Small streams and rivers begin on high land where rain falls. Small rivers and streams rush down hills and mountains and eventually join together to make larger rivers that flow to the sea.

☐ When the sun shines through falling rain we see rainbows. The colours in a rainbow are red, orange yellow, green, blue, indigo, violet.

Picture points

1 The rain is falling from a big cloud, but the sun is shining through the raindrops and so we can see beautiful colours in the rainbow. Let's look in the border and see all the colours.

2 There are clouds near the mountains, but it's sunny on the shore. Show me the places where it's sunny.

3 What a lot of water there is in our picture – little streams, rivers, and the sea. Show me them all.

4 People have fun near water. Can you see the people canoeing and the picnickers? What else are people doing?

5 How many things can you see being moved by the wind? (Glider, balloon, sailing boats, clouds, trees.) Is it a strong wind? Which way is it blowing?

6 Why do you think the little white house by the river has a large wheel fixed to it? (It's an old mill.)

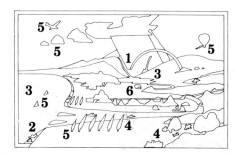

Talking Points

1 How many things in this picture have you seen yourself? Have you ever seen a rainbow? (Who were you with when you saw it? Where was it?)

2 Where is it raining in the picture? Do you think the people in the balloon are getting wet?

3 Why is so much water pouring down the hills? (Rain falls on high land.) Then where does it go? (Waterfall, lake, river, sea.)

4 If you could have any sort of weather you wanted, what sort of weather would you choose to have? Do you like rain? If it didn't rain rain, what would you like to come down instead? Sweets? Chocolate drops? Sausages?

Learning Skills

Memory
Children are unlikely to remember that it rained on a particular day ("on Tuesday" for instance), but they will remember that rain affected something they were doing. Use this fact to help exercise their memories.
☐ Let's try and remember when it rained last. Did it rain this morning? Or yesterday? Or the day before that when we went to ....? Did it rain last time we went shopping, or when we went to see Granny? (And so on.)
☐ It's a long time (or not very long) since it rained, isn't it?
☐ Do you remember if there's been a big thunderstorm (or snow or something else rare) lately? What were we doing then? What do we usually do when it snows? When it's sunny?

What weather does
Children can gradually learn that weather affects people in different ways.
☐ Look again at the picture. The raincloud is blowing over the land.
☐ Who will be upset if the cloud goes over them? (Sunbathers, picnickers.) What will they have to do? (Pack up, take shelter.) Who might be quite glad? (Farmer.)
☐ Who is glad when the wind blows? (Dinghy sailors.) Who might be upset? (People with parasols.)
☐ Suppose the wind was really strong, who would be frightened? (Balloonists.)
Story and games on p.58

Islands

*This picture helps children to under-
stand what an island is and will also
help older children to realize that where
they live closely affects the life they lead.*

☐ An island is a piece of land that has
water all around it. You can't get to the
island without crossing the water.

☐ People who live on an island are
often good sailors and fishermen.

☐ Any food the islanders can't grow or
catch has to be brought across the sea.

☐ We can visit islands when we are on
holiday and we often find that life on
the island is very different from home.

Picture points

1 To get to this island you would
probably come by boat. Can you see the
place where a boat could unload its
passengers? Can you see where smaller
boats can land?

2 The island is quite small, so you never
have to travel very far. There's a man
who hires out bikes to visitors so they
can get around quickly.

3 The donkey is just going off round the
road. How many other ways of going
around the island can you see? (Bus,
bike, car, foot.)

4 That's a big church for such a small
island. What could you see if you
climbed right up the tower? (All over
the island, out to sea, the mainland,
other islands.)

5 The fishing nets have to be mended
carefully. What do you think happens if
the holes are too big?

6 Can you find some tiny islands in the
sea? They are too small for people to
live on, but some sea birds may live and
nest on them.

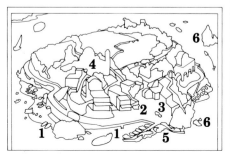

Talking Points

1 There is an old ruin up on one of the hills. I wonder what it used to be.

2 There are quite a few different animals kept on this island. Why do you think a goat is useful? And a donkey?

3 Some of the people in the picture are on holiday, but most of them live and work on the island. What sort of work do you think people would do here? (Fishing, farming, hotel work, etc.)

4 Some of the people are staying on the island for their holiday. How do you think they spend their time here? Which building do you think they stay in?

Learning Skills

Ways of doing things
There are often many different ways of doing things, and we can talk about the advantages and disadvantages of each. This is a good picture for showing that we can travel in many different ways. Older children can begin to assess the relative merits of each form of transport.
☐ Wouldn't it be fun to go all round this island on the water?
☐ How many different ways of doing that can you show me?
☐ Which one would be quickest/ slowest/best if you wanted to look at everything carefully, etc?
☐ Suppose you were having a race round the island. Which way would you choose? What disasters might happen to slow you down? (Run out of petrol, hit rock, sudden storm, etc.)

Viewpoints
Children don't find it easy to work out that other people can see things that they can't. This exercise is difficult but worth trying with older children.
☐ Do you see the people sitting outside the café? Can they see the harbour? The bus? The donkey in front of the bus? The church? Which boats can they not see? Can the people on the big cruiser over there see the café? When will they be able to? Show me where their boat will be then.
☐ Why do you think the castle was at the top of the island with a good view all round? What do you think might be on the other side of the island, which we can't see from our position?
Story and games on p.59

Jungles

The South American jungle is one of the many parts of the world that have still not been thoroughly explored. This picture introduces a few of the exciting aspects of exploration.

☐ People cannot travel easily through the jungle and rivers often make the best "roads".

☐ Explorers come to find out about the animals, plants, people and minerals in the jungle. They usually work with guides, who know the country and how to look after yourself there.

☐ Explorers need to take a great deal of equipment both for their work and to help them live in the jungle.

Picture points

1 The explorers have come up the river in two boats. Which boat got here first? Who was in it?

2 The guides are leading the way. They are cutting a path through the thick plants with their sharp knives. The guides know all about the jungle.

3 The people in the second boat are un-loading the explorers' luggage. Then they will start to make a camp.

4 There's someone with a very special job. He's making a film of everything that happens. Do you think you might ever see his film? (Maybe on TV.)

5 Let's point to all the animals and birds. What do you think they will do when they see the explorers? (Run away, hide. They don't usually attack!)

6 The explorers have to wear comfort-able clothes. Are they wearing sensible clothes or not? (Yes, but their legs and arms may get scratched or bitten by insects. Perhaps they need hats.)

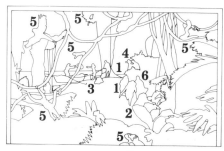

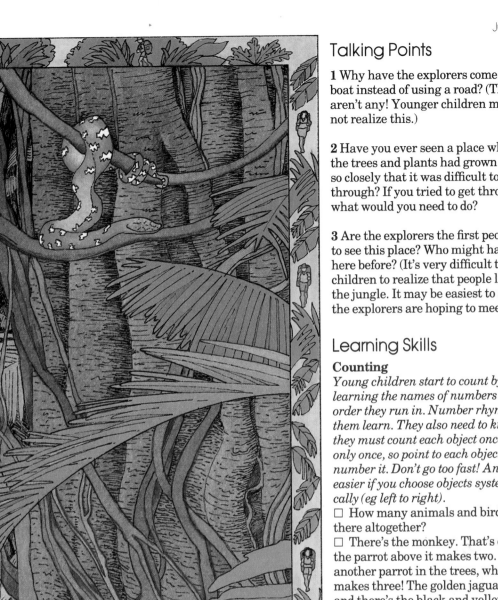

Talking Points

1 Why have the explorers come in a boat instead of using a road? (There aren't any! Younger children may well not realize this.)

2 Have you ever seen a place where the trees and plants had grown together so closely that it was difficult to get through? If you tried to get through, what would you need to do?

3 Are the explorers the first people ever to see this place? Who might have been here before? (It's very difficult to help children to realize that people live in the jungle. It may be easiest to say that the explorers are hoping to meet them.)

Learning Skills

Counting

Young children start to count by learning the names of numbers and the order they run in. Number rhymes help them learn. They also need to know that they must count each object once and only once, so point to each object as you number it. Don't go too fast! And it is easier if you choose objects systematically (eg left to right).

☐ How many animals and birds are there altogether?

☐ There's the monkey. That's one and the parrot above it makes two. There's another parrot in the trees, which makes three! The golden jaguar is four and there's the black and yellow frog – five. Then there's the snake up in the tree. That's six.

☐ So there are six animals altogether, aren't there?

Don't expect instant success. It will help if you have some toy animals to hand, so that your child has an object to touch as you count together.

What exploring is

Once your child begins to understand what the explorers are doing, you can lead on to the much more difficult question of why they are doing it.

☐ What do you think is nice about exploring? (Adventure, new places, exciting animals, etc.)

☐ What might not be so nice? (Heat, insect bites, strange food.)

☐ How do the explorers tell us about the places they find? (Books, films.)

☐ Where would you like to explore?

Story and games on p.60

LANDMARKS

Mountain Tops

Mountains and caves are the highest and lowest places we can reach. This picture also helps children to think about the important idea that things look different from different viewpoints.

☐ Mountaineers enjoy trying to get to the summit of a rock or mountain. They usually climb in groups so they can help one another. They wear climbing clothes and carry special equipment.

☐ When you get to the top of a mountain you can see a very long way and you can see what's on the other side. People on the ground think you look very small when you are on top.

☐ The higher you go, the colder it gets. Snow and ice often form on the peaks.

Picture points

1 How is the man at the top helping the man just below him? (Holding him secure on the rope, guiding him.)

2 The climbers have iron spikes called crampons on the bottom of their boots. They also have special axes. What are they for? (To grip the snow/ice.)

3 Why are the climbers wearing goggles? (Eyes can be damaged by the sun shining on the glistening snow.)

4 Climbers use special fasteners on their ropes. (See border.)

5 The ground between the two lines of mountains is called a valley. It is warmer in the valley because it is protected by the sides of the mountains and it's much lower down. You can see there is no snow in the valley.

6 You can go up some popular mountains on a special railway.

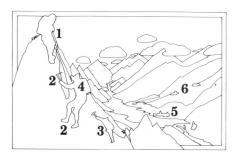

Talking Points

1 Do you know where the highest place near home is? Have you been to the top? What can you see when you get there?

2 How can you tell the mountain is a high one? (Snow.) Why do you think the village looks so small? (Because it's much lower down and a long way away.)

Learning Skills

Up and down
Words like up and down, over and under, etc, are important, for they point out the relationships of things to each other in space.

☐ Look at those people climbing up the mountain. Who is nearest the top? And so who is farthest up? Who is coming up next? Who is going to get up last? And who is farthest down?

☐ Could anyone get even farther up than the man on top? (Only if they were flying.)

☐ If the man on the top sat down on his bottom and started sliding where would he go? How far down would he get? Would he go lower than the last man climbing up? Then who would be farthest down?

How we see things
Children learn in infancy to make allowances for distance when judging the size of things. But it is quite another matter for them to be consciously aware that they are doing so. They find it even harder to imagine what things must look like from another person's viewpoint.

☐ Pretend you are sitting down in the village looking up at the mountain top and one of the climbers is Dad. He's the one in the bright red clothes. Can you see him? What does he look like? (Very, very small.) Could you use anything to help you see him? (Telescope.)

☐ Could Dad see you? What would you look like?

☐ Now imagine you are right away on the other side of the mountain. Could you see Dad climbing? (Only when he got right to the top.) What could Dad do to show you he'd got to the top? (Wave, put up a flag.) (Your child probably needs to be quite old before he even begins to understand this; so don't force it, it's difficult. The game (on p.61) is an easier way of tackling the same problem successfully.)
Story and games on p.61

LANDMARKS

Deep Caves

Mountains are fairly easy for children to understand, but the idea that there are huge holes underground that we can explore needs a careful introduction to children who have never seen one.

☐ The huge caves deep down in the earth have usually been made by water. They are full of strange shapes, exciting colours and mysterious tunnels.

☐ Some caves are so interesting and famous that people visit them all through the year.

☐ Potholers enjoy exploring new caves, but potholing is difficult and dangerous and so not a hobby for children. (They should be warned never to go inside any cave without an adult.)

Picture points

1 There are underground caves in many parts of the world. They can be huge or tiny. This one is so big that we can't even see it all. It's bigger than a house!

2 Can you see the people who have just entered the dark cave? What's that behind them? (Daylight.)

3 Can you see the things that have been done to help visitors see the cave? (Stairs, lights, boats, guides.)

4 Those people are going on a mystery boat ride deep underground. The guide has a very strong torch to help them see all the shapes and patterns in the rock.

5 Deep underground you sometimes find these pointed shapes. The ones hanging down are called stalactites and the ones pointing up are called stalagmites. Show me some of each.

6 The potholers in the rubber dinghy are going off to see if they can discover a new cave.

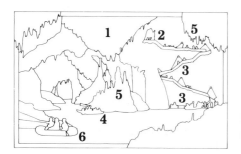

Talking Points

1 Can you see what the potholers have with them to help them explore? (Torches, map, rope, boat, etc.)

2 There are so many strange shapes that it looks as if people made them, doesn't it? But they didn't. Do you know what did? (Underground rivers washed away at the rock for years and years and made the cave, very, very slowly. See Study Box on p.62.) What things in the cave have been made by people to help visitors see round? (Stairs, railings, lights, boats.)

3 There are hardly any animals or birds deep underground, so it's very quiet. What noises do you think you might hear there? (Echoes, slowly moving water, drips falling.)

Learning Skills

What would you need?
Children don't often plan ahead and so it is important to encourage them to do so whenever you have a chance.
☐ Imagine you are going to visit a cave on a warm sunny day. What would you need to take with you?
☐ What would you wear? Would you take a thick jumper? (Remind your child that there's no sun underground. It's cold and often damp and slippery.)
☐ What would you take to help you see if all the lights went out?
☐ What else would you take? (Possible ideas are some food, extra clothes, etc.)

What things are for
The exercise above helps children plan for themselves. This exercise introduces the much harder task of thinking for other people.
☐ Now let's look very carefully at the potholers in the rubber dinghy.
☐ What are they wearing? Why have they got rubber suits on? (Stop them getting wet, keep them warm.)
☐ Would they ever go swimming in those suits? (Yes, if the tunnel got very narrow.) Then what would they need? (Masks, oxygen tanks, flippers.)
☐ Why do you think they've all got hard hats on? (In case they bang their heads on a stalactite or rock.)
☐ Would they need anything else? What might they use a rope for? (Tying up boat, climbing in cave, etc.)
Story and games on p.62

The Sea Bed

Very few young children have had the opportunity of looking at the world under the sea except on television programmes. They can learn that an exciting world exists down there.

☐ Sunken ships rest on reefs, rocks and the sea bed. They gradually break up, although they can be preserved in mud.

☐ People dive down from ships and use special clothes and equipment to explore underwater and find treasure.

☐ Submarines move underwater with engines, and use lights and cameras to help the explorers.

☐ Many sea plants and fish live on or near old sunken ships like this one.

Picture points

1 The divers have discovered the remains of a very old ship. What things have they found in it? (Cannon, treasure.) Some of the old things are stuck in the mud; the divers work together to get them out.

2 The people in the submarine help the divers with their lights. The lights need to be very strong because it is dark deep underwater.

3 It is very difficult to hear under water. All the divers hear is the sound of air bubbling up from their tanks.

4 Ships on top of the water lift the treasure up when the divers give a signal. The divers can tie floats to their finds so they bob up to the surface.

5 The big pipe sucks mud away and then the diver uses a metal detector to find if any treasure has been uncovered.

6 Fish are not very frightened of the divers. They come very close and (apart from the shark) are friendly.

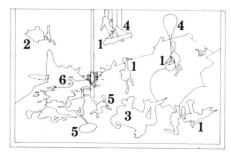

Talking Points

1 How many divers are there? Why do you think they wear a rubber suit? (For warmth.) A mask? (To see clearly.) Flippers? (To swim more easily.) Tanks on their backs? (To hold their air supply.)

2 Are all the fish the same shape? Point to the fiercest-looking. Can you see what we call a shoal of fish?

3 Look at the things the divers have found (in the border). Can you guess what they are and where they came from? I wonder why the ship sank? (Storm? Rocks? Sunk in a battle?)

4 Would you like to be a diver or one of the people in the submarine?

5 There are lots of bubbles round the divers. What are they? (Air.) Where are they coming from? (Special tanks.)

Learning Skills

What things are for

You will have talked about the divers' equipment already but it's worth concentrating on it and, as you do so, helping your child to understand more about underwater conditions.

☐ What is the diver's rubber suit for? It helps keep him warm doesn't it? (So it's cold underwater – there is no warmth from the sun down there.)

☐ Why does he have a special mask and a tank? (You can't breathe underwater because you would just suck in water. Fish can get air out of water.)

☐ What are his flippers for? (Deep water makes movement difficult.)

☐ Why does he have a knife in the sheath on his leg? (To prise things off rocks, clear mud from finds, etc.)

Let's imagine

You can often find out how well children understand things by asking them to pretend they are in that situation – in this case, swimming along underwater.

☐ What does the suit feel like? (Quite warm and comfy.)

☐ What can you hear? (Hiss of air, muffled sounds. Everything must seem very noisy when you get back on land.)

☐ What can you feel? (Water, but the suit keeps your body dry.)

☐ Now you swim round the corner and suddenly you see a . . .

Story and games on p.63

Greek Wedding

Weddings are celebrated in very different ways in each country, but all weddings bring whole families together to help make the day a memorable one.

☐ When two people get married they agree to become husband and wife. Everyone comes to their wedding to wish them happiness and luck.

☐ Every country has special customs at weddings. Children are often very involved in these.

☐ The bride, groom and their attendants usually wear special clothes.

☐ Food, drink, music and gift-giving are important parts of most wedding celebrations all over the world.

Picture points

1 A woman (the bride) and a man (the bridegroom) have just got married in the church. Now they are having a party with their friends. The bride is wearing a white dress and the bridegroom a smart traditional costume. Can you see them?

2 Look, the bride and groom have got money pinned on their clothes! Their friends pinned it on to help them buy things for the new home that they will live in together now they are married.

3 The girls in the long dresses with white aprons are the bridesmaids, who help the bride. How many are there?

4 Everyone is happy. They are laughing and clapping and singing and dancing. Can you see the things they are eating?

5 Can you see the musicians? They are playing a fiddle, a tambourine and a mandola. Some of the guests are clapping in time to the music.

Talking Points

1 What sort of things do you think the bride and the bridegroom will buy with the money pinned to them?

2 How can we tell these people live in a warm, sunny land where it doesn't rain too often? (Plants, sky, clothes, party outside, blue sky.)

3 Do you think the wedding party has just begun, or is it towards the end? (End, they have almost finished eating.)

Learning Skills

Sounds

Different musical instruments make different sounds and need to be played in different ways. You can help children to learn this by making very simple instruments: try stretching elastic bands across a box and plucking them, etc.

☐ Can you see the instrument for tapping and shaking? Do you know its name? (Tambourine.)

☐ Can you see the instruments with strings? Do you know what they are? (Mandola, fiddle.)

☐ One is being strummed. The player is moving his hand across the strings. What sort of noise does he make?

☐ Can you see any people making sounds without using any musical instruments? (Everyone clapping.) Are they making music or not? (Clapping in time adds to rhythm of dance.)

☐ Do you know how the players with string instruments make the sound higher or lower? (Make strings shorter or longer by changing position of fingers. Show how with elastic bands.)

Other people's feelings

Begin by suggesting that all the people in the picture like each other and are happy together. Then move on to why it is nice to be with other people.

☐ What do other people do to help you and make you happy? (Food, clothes, housekeeping, treats, play.)

☐ Who does these nice things for children? (Parents, relatives, friends.)

☐ Who does them for grown-ups? (Still parents and relatives [less] and friends [more], although grown-ups also have to look after themselves.)

☐ When people grow up they often get married and have one particular special person to help and make happy.

Story and games on p.64

CELEBRATIONS

A Japanese Ceremony

Some festivals celebrate growing up, and this is one of them. Children can realize that several different people in their families care about them and are interested in their development.

☐ Some festivals, such as this Japanese one, are special times for children.

☐ Japanese families put on their best clothes – traditional or modern – and go to the shrines to celebrate their children's health and future.

☐ When whole families gather together there are many complicated relationships to understand.

Picture points

1 This special day happens when children are three, five and seven years old. Who do you think is three, five or seven? People say "thank you" at the shrine by putting their hands together and praying.

2 Can you see what this gateway is decorated with? (Plaited rope, strips of paper and knotted straw. These signify an area of sanctity and purity.)

3 Some little girls and ladies are wearing olden-day clothes called kimonos. These are mostly worn on special days.

4 After the ceremony families meet their friends outside the temple and chat and laugh with them.

5 The children have been given fancy bags of sweets for this special day.

6 Uncle is taking the family photograph. Mum and Dad will keep the photograph to show how well and happy their children were on that day. Can you see Granny and Grandad?

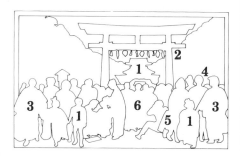

Talking Points

1 Families are made up of children, mums, dads, aunts, uncles, cousins, and grannies and grandads. Families often only meet all together when something important happens. When did we all meet as a family? Can you remember? (Wedding, christening, birthday.)

2 What sorts of things do families do when they meet on an important day? (Eat special food, drink special drinks, wear best clothes, take photographs.)

Learning Skills

Other people's feelings
The picture is a good one for helping your child to learn that he can work out what other people may feel by remembering what he felt like in a similar situation.
☐ Look at all the children dressed in their best clothes and being very good. What do you think they feel like? (Rather strange, awkward, proud, etc.)
☐ Show me someone who is happy. How do you know they are? Are they smiling?
☐ Can you see someone who isn't happy at the moment? What do you think made her cry? (Too many people, accident, etc.) Do you think she'll soon be smiling again?
☐ Can you see someone who is a bit shy? What is she doing to make herself feel better? (Hanging on to her mum!)
☐ Now look at all the mums and dads. How do you think they are feeling?

Same and different
In this picture there are good opportunities for talking about "same" and "different", using clothes as examples.
☐ Can you see some people whose clothes are nearly exactly the same? (The men.)
☐ Who has clothes that are very different from the men's? (The women in traditional dress.) What are the differences? (Much more colourful, voluminous, beautiful, etc.)
☐ Are the kimonos all the same? (No, differences in colour, pattern.)
☐ Can you see any ladies who are not wearing a kimono? Their clothes are really smart too aren't they?
☐ I think I can see something that is the same for all the ladies in kimonos, can you? (Socks and sandals.)
Story and games on p.65

CELEBRATIONS

A Folk Dance

Traditional folk dances are performed at special times of year in many countries. The performers bring great skill to their dancing, costume-making and music even though they may no longer believe that the dance has magical powers.

☐ In many African villages, men, women and children enjoy dancing.

☐ In this rain-making dance there is a great deal of clapping, singing, dancing, drumming and dressing up.

☐ The men who play the instruments are the band. They go on and on playing all the time and everyone else joins in with the rhythm.

☐ Usually when dancers dress up they are pretending to be someone else.

Picture points

1 Isn't this a big party? Everyone seems to be having fun. Can you spot any children having a happy time? What are they doing?

2 How many men are there in the band? What kind of noise do you think each of the instruments makes? Which instrument would you like to be playing?

3 Can you see the dancer? Would you like to dress up in a mask and strange clothes like that? He is pretending to be a butterfly. Do you think he looks at all like a butterfly?

4 The butterfly dancer is shivering his wings to show he feels the first drops of rain. Does it look as if it's really going to rain? Perhaps he hasn't danced enough yet! The drummer will lead him through the village to a special dancing place in a clearing.

5 Have you noticed the houses these people live in? They are made from mud bricks baked in the sun.

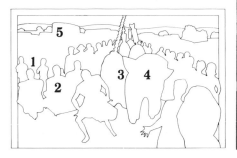

Talking Points

1 Everyone is singing and dancing because they hope it will rain soon and they need water for their plants and animals. Will their dance make it rain? (No. But they are likely to perform it at a time of year when it may soon do so.)

2 Is the butterfly dancer an adult or child? (He is an adult because a child would not be able to dance such a difficult dance.)

3 Where do you think the musicians get their splendid drums and other instruments? (They are made by themselves or by local craftsmen.)

Learning Skills

What things are made of

Children don't always realize that materials which they see in everyday use can be used in many other exciting ways. Equally, many everyday objects can be made out of very unlikely materials.

□ Did you know that we can use wood to make musical instruments? Which of the instruments are made from wood? (Xylophone, flutes.) Do you know what they would sound like?

□ What other instruments do you know that are made with wood? (Violin, piano, guitar, castanets, etc.)

□ Let's look at the butterfly dancer. What's his costume made from? (Grass, reeds, natural materials.)

□ Could we make a costume out of natural materials? What would we use? How would we fit them together? How would we fit them on to our bodies?

Rhythm

Rhythm is an important and simple musical sense. Explain it by talking through these questions, then go on to the game on p.66.

□ Let's look at the dancer, the band and the audience very carefully. Are all the musicians doing the same thing? (No. Some blow, some hit.)

□ Which musician is beating the time? (Drummer.) Which are playing a tune? (Flute and xylophone players, singers.)

□ What are the audience doing? (Clapping in time to the drum.) They are helping the dancer to dance well.

□ What does the dancer have to do? (Move head, arms and feet in time.)

□ Could you dance in time if I clap?

Story and games on p.66

CELEBRATIONS

Midsummer Festival

Festivals can be landmarks in children's lives. They help them get a grasp of the year's sequence; they make them feel part of the community; and they give them something to look forward to.

☐ Every country has its own special days at various times of year. These days are called festivals.

☐ This picture shows people in Sweden celebrating the festival of midsummer. The dark, cold winter has passed, the spring has made things grow and now the warm sun is shining down.

☐ People often use flowers and plants as decorations and wear their country's traditional clothes to celebrate.

☐ Not many people work on a festival day: everybody enjoys themselves.

Picture points

1 These people in Sweden have got a lovely summer's day for their festival. They are dancing around a large pole, which they have decorated with flowers, ribbons and leaves.

2 Some people just want to watch and enjoy the fun. They help the dancers by clapping to the music.

3 Other people play music at the festival. They play different instruments together. Show me an accordion player.

4 Children have come with their families and friends to watch the fun. I expect some of them may join the dancers. Can you see two of the children who are trying to practise?

5 Some of the girls are wearing pretty garlands of flowers on their heads. They have made these themselves from flowers growing in the fields.

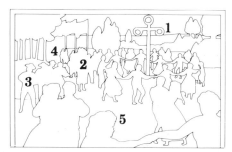

Talking Points

1 Look at the people who are wearing clothes like Swedish people wore long ago. How do they look different from the people wearing ordinary clothes?

2 We have festivals and holidays when we have fun and enjoy ourselves. Can you think of some of the special days we have? How do we celebrate? What sorts of things do we do? Do we use flowers as decorations at any of them?

3 Can you think of any other costumes that people from a different country wear at festivals?

Learning Skills

How do we dance?
Many children find dancing an exciting way to express their emotions. Young children start by moving in time to music. You can help to lead them on by talking through what they are doing.
☐ What do you have to do first when you are starting a dance? (Listen to music, decide what you feel like.)
☐ Then you start moving. Can your feet dance? Can your hands and arms dance? Can your head dance? Can your whole body dance?
☐ What do you have to do to dance with someone else? Do you hold hands or just stand opposite them? Do you have to watch what they are doing or not?
☐ What about dancing with lots of people like the dancers in the picture? How do you do that? How do you all keep together in a circle?

What people are doing
It is quite hard for younger children to manage to move together and keep time when they are dancing in a group. It's worth talking this through before you go outside to practise.
☐ Which people are playing musical instruments? What would happen if one person played the tune very fast and another one very slowly? (You could try this with a well-known tune.) It sounds funny, doesn't it?
☐ Who else in the picture needs to do things in time with the musicians? (The dancers, who have to keep in step; the people clapping to the music.)
☐ What kind of music is best for dancing? (Something with a strong beat.) Is that the kind you like best?
Story and games on p.67

CELEBRATIONS

Carnival

Colour and rhythm are the keynotes of this carnival. All the hard work of making the costumes and practising the music and dancing is forgotten when the big day finally arrives.

☐ The annual carnival in Trinidad is one of the most exciting and colourful celebrations in the world. All the islanders come out to watch.

☐ People spend months together preparing and planning the magnificent costumes for their group.

☐ Each group has a band and a king and a queen.

☐ Before the carnival march, competitions are held to find the best band, the best calypso singer and the best kings and queens.

Picture points

1 Here come the sea creatures down the street. They have planned their costumes and made them very carefully so that they match each other. Do you think those big fishing spears are real ones or not?

2 The band are drumming out a tune on their steel drums. It makes everybody want to dance. Even the players in the band look as if they might start dancing at any minute.

3 The birds are coming along behind the band. Can you see the King of the Birds in his magnificent costume? Do you like his mask?

4 Children have a separate carnival of their own, but some of them have put their costumes on again so they can run along beside the parade.

5 What's the best way to make sure you see everything? Who is sitting high above the crowd?

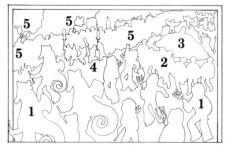

Talking Points

1 Each group chooses one idea for their costumes. In the competition they are judged on how well their costumes match that idea. Who would you give the prize to, the birds or the fish?

2 There are brass bands and calypso groups as well as steel bands in the parade. Can you imagine what they all sound like? What can the people in the crowd do to join in with the music? (Sing, clap in time, have a dance.)

3 I wonder who is going to get hottest in the bright sunshine? Who has made sure they will keep quite cool?

Learning Skills

Memory
You can use most of the pictures in the book for simple memory exercises, but younger children will find pictures that have a very clear progression in them easier to manage. Tell your child what you are going to do, let him have a last look, then shut the book.
☐ Where was the procession going? (Through the streets of Trinidad.)
☐ What were the two groups of dancers dressed up as? Were the birds or the fish in front? What were the fish carrying?
☐ Was there anyone in between the birds and the fish? (Give a hint if you need to, "I think they were making a noise," etc.)
☐ Who was running along beside the procession? What were they wearing?

Planning ahead
It's good for children to realize that happy, carefree events such as this one need enormously careful planning, but you need to separate out each action to help them do so.
☐ Long before Carnival time, what did each group have to do? (Decide what they wanted to be.)
☐ Then what did they have to do? (Plan costumes so they all match each other.)
☐ Then they had to measure everyone and make the costumes didn't they? And then? (Try them on, practise dancing in them.)
☐ While the costumes were being made, what did the band do? (Make up tunes and learn to play them.)
☐ What did the band and the dancers have to do together? (Practise.)
Story and games on p.68

Chinese New Year

Many communities have exciting and colourful celebrations to mark New Year. The Chinese New Year, celebrated for two whole weeks in February, is a stimulating example of how people make a fresh start when the old year ends.

□ The highlight of the Chinese New Year takes place outside and all the streets are colourfully decorated.

□ The dragon dance is an important part of the celebrations as the dragon is said to bring good luck.

□ Everyone makes a fresh start to the year by being friendly, by giving presents and by remembering things that happened in the old year.

Picture points

1 The dragon is really a huge costume very carefully made.

2 The dragon's head is carved from wood and painted. Its body is made with bright cloth over a wire frame.

3 Men and big boys go right underneath the frame so that you can hardly see them, and so the dragon looks alive.

4 The man inside the dragon's head can move it up and down and from side to side so that the dragon looks lively.

5 The musicians play drums and gongs to help the dancers under the dragon to move in time with each other.

6 The leader carries the long pole with decorations of paper, pompoms and bells on top to show the dragon the way.

7 The lanterns are made of paper on a frame; the light shines through the paper so you can see the lovely designs.

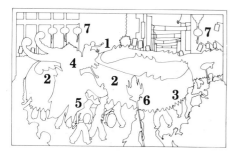

Talking Points

1 Little red envelopes with money in them are being given to people as presents. Can you see anyone who has been given a present?

2 Chinese people have their own way of writing, which you can see on the banners and in the border. What do you think the writing says? (Happy New Year. Prosperity and good luck. May you have the energy and stamina of the dragon and the horse. May you have money and wealth.)

Learning Skills

Where things are
Children need a good deal of practice with the important words that show position, but you need to present the questions in an enjoyable way. Try to show them that there are always two ways to look at each position: "If I am in front of you then you are behind me," and so on.

☐ Can you see all the banners and lanterns hanging up high above the street? Show me the ones you like best. Which looks highest? How did they get up there?

☐ Show me the man in front of the procession. Who is behind him? What are they in front of? Who is the dragon behind?

☐ Who is under the dragon? What do you think it is like in there? (Dark or light? Quiet or noisy?)

How to do a dragon dance
Dragon dancers are highly skilled and move very quickly. You can't expect children to be as skilled as the experts, but practising together as a group is worthwhile.

☐ How do the dancers make the dragon move? (Yes, they all run along twisting and turning.)

☐ How do you think they make sure they all keep going the same way? (They watch the person in front and listen to signals from the musicians.)

☐ Could you do a dragon dance with your friends? Why not choose a leader. Put your hands on her shoulders. The next person puts hands on your shoulders, and so on. One, two, three, off we go. (Encourage the leader to make the line as wiggly as possible. Change leaders so everyone has a turn.)
Story and games on p.69

CELEBRATIONS

International Village

Sometimes people from different parts of the world meet for special purposes. This picture shows your children an example – an international village, one of several organized every summer to bring children from different countries together.

☐ People from different countries can be friends, even if they speak different languages.

☐ People everywhere can find some activity to share and enjoy.

☐ In most countries, people wear special clothes for celebrations. These are often like ones worn long ago.

☐ People look different according to the countries they come from.

Picture points

1 These children come from many different countries. How can you tell that? (Dress, features.)

2 Where have all the children come from? (Starting with the adult in the middle of the picture and working clockwise), these people come from Guatemala (camp leader), France, Nigeria, Germany, USA, India, Netherlands, Scotland, Switzerland (camp leader), Italy, Mexico, Japan, Norway (camp leader), Nigeria, USA, Netherlands. (From bottom left), the flags in the border are: Spain, Argentina, Indonesia, Britain, Italy, Austria, Finland, India, France, Nigeria, Norway, Guatemala, Netherlands, Mexico, USA, Japan, West Germany.

3 The children are having a party at the end of their holiday together. What are they doing? (Singing, dancing, playing musical instruments.) Which would you be doing, if you were one of them?

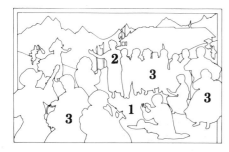

Talking Points

1 Which clothes would you take to an international village for a national costume party?

2 All the children have been on holiday together for a month. Which children do you think have made friends together during the holiday?

3 Do you think it would be fun to have a friend from another country? How would you keep in touch with each other? (Writing, postcards, visits, etc.)

Learning Skills

How to talk to foreigners
The best way to practise this idea is to pretend you only speak a foreign language and see what your child can do. Children are often extremely inventive in this kind of work.

☐ When the children first meet at the village, they often only speak their own language. Imagine you had just arrived at the village.

☐ How would you say "hello"?

☐ How would you tell everyone your name? How would you find out theirs?

☐ How would you ask them where to find the bedrooms, etc? How would you show them where to go?

☐ How would you start cooking (or any other activity) together?

☐ How quickly do you think you could learn their language and start having conversations with them?

Other people's feelings
This last picture presents a number of difficult ideas. Younger children may simply enjoy the colourful costumes, but older children can begin to think about the emotions involved.

☐ All the children are wearing special clothes. Are they their party clothes or are they even more special than that? What do they feel like in them?

☐ The clothes show which country they belong to. When do we have special feelings about our country? (At sporting fixtures, etc; often when we go abroad.)

☐ Two of the children are wearing clothes which show that they belong to a group of people who live in a country with many other people (the Scot and the American Indian). How do you think they feel? (Often especially proud and, sometimes, sensitive.)

Story and games on p.70

— Checking Progress —

Is your child learning?

You can't test how well your child is doing in this kind of work because it is impossible to make a test that has any real value and, in any case, the whole process of deliberately testing a young child is more than likely to put him off working with you at all. However, if the work is going well, he will be acquiring and beginning to use new vocabulary, mastering all kinds of thinking skills, greatly increasing his manual and physical dexterity and be giving evidence of this in everything he does. Of course this only happens very gradually and you will probably want to pause now and then to see how things are going.

Keeping a record

The best way to record progress is to choose two or three of the pictures that seem to be your child's favourites and keep notes of what he does and says each time he looks at those pictures. You may not come back to them very frequently and so you may well find that you had not realized just how much more he has thought out from one session with a picture to the next. If you are really interested in your child's development you could add photographs of the models he makes or the games he plays to produce a small, very personal scrapbook. No doubt your child will enjoy helping you to keep it up to date.

Things to watch for

Concentration How long did your child concentrate on a picture? What sort of things distract him? What helps him to concentrate? Small children can quite easily be distracted by things going on around them, particularly when they're not sure what it is they are supposed to be doing. They'll show more interest and concentrate better if they understand the aim of the activity, can cope with its demands, and are receiving your support and praise when they try hard and do well. It's also important to concentrate yourself so that they can use you as a model for learning how to set about things.

Success Children, like the rest of us, enjoy success and dislike failing. They can also tell the difference between deserved praise and being fobbed off with "Oh, that's nice dear." So learning is most enjoyable when questions and problems can be dealt with successfully with a little bit of effort, and when they offer an opportunity to show off cleverness to an admiring public. This means you need to organize your questions so that there are some the child can answer straight off, some that he can do with a little help from you, and none, or almost none, that he can't begin to manage. You know a lot about your child, which is the first step, and you can note what makes questions easier or harder for him. If he's being right all the time very easily you may like to try a few harder ideas – questions beginning "how" and "why" are usually more difficult than those beginning "what" or "who". If he's having difficulties, make things a bit easier, use simpler questions, half give the answer, and so on. Don't get upset if your child gives the "wrong" answer. Anybody who's "right" all the time won't learn anything new, after all.

General conversation Does he know the names of all the objects in the picture? Are there any he doesn't know? Can you explain them easily to him? Are you able to talk about them for long enough to hear him using them correctly again later? Encourage your child to do his fair share of talking and avoid dominating the conversation yourself. It's important to give the child time and space to express his own ideas, and you will be able to judge how fast he is learning by how long he wants the conversation to continue. Picture Points and Talking Points: Does he talk about all the points? Does he talk about anything you have done together which related to one of the picture points?

Learning Skills How many of the questions can your child manage and how long do you take to talk about each question? Which sorts of questions went well and which badly? How important is it for your child that you and he take turns being the questioner? In general, the longer he wants, the more he is learning.

Playing When your child starts playing, do you happen to hear any of the things you were talking about come out again? Could you link this into your next session with the pictures? Could you extend it with a visit to an appropriate place – castle, beach, museum, supermarket, roadworks or whatever?

Warning Perhaps the most important point is that if your child is not enjoying his sessions with you and the books he probably won't learn anything that will do him much good. The same will be true if you're not enjoying it. It is quite possible to train your child to do all sorts of things he doesn't really want to do and to force yourself through the agonies of doing so. It is very doubtful whether either of you will gain much by this.

Reading And Counting

Between the ages of three and six your child will start simple counting and is quite likely to start wanting to read. Like every other parent, you will probably be torn between wanting to teach your child more, worrying that he does not seem to be as advanced as the last child you met, and fearing that whatever you do may conflict with what the teachers will do when your child reaches school.

The Let's Learn Method

The *Let's Learn* books offer you a middle road between these various pitfalls. In the first place, they will help you to get your child ready to learn. As you share these books, your child will be learning in a thoroughly enjoyable way and will, quite automatically, want to get more involved. Secondly, you should realize that children acquire all intellectual skills very gradually and that no two children gain them in exactly the same order. These books help you to build on your child's strengths and successes and so help him to develop in an entirely natural way.

Starting to read

The best way you can help your child to begin reading is to make sure that he speaks his language fluently and understands what's said to him. He will then be far more likely to attach the appropriate meaning to the words and sentences he will find in reading books. There are other activities that are helpful before your child learns to read properly and many of these have been suggested at various places in the books. He will probably begin to recognize words that you may have pointed out to him, for example, the names of shops. Play as many word-spotting games as you like; spotting words that already mean things to him is much easier for your child than recognizing single letters, which can mean very little. If your child falls naturally into reading, then encourage him to carry on, but don't worry if he doesn't

Counting

Teaching children numbers is at least as worthwhile as helping them to start reading. A range of early number skills that you can perfectly well practise and develop have been suggested through the books. Children who have plenty of practice in the kind of skills suggested will find arithmetic and maths easier when they get to school, regardless of whether they are taught by the traditional methods or by the so-called "new maths".

Once your child has started coming to grips with the ideas in a picture, he needs to start exploring them in ways that are not just factual or intended to help him acquire solid information. He needs to play with the ideas, perhaps build fantasies round them and, whenever possible, explore them through his own activity. Some of the ideas in these pages may prove so easy for your child that they fail to interest him; others may be beyond him at present. You should be able to adapt most of them to suit your child's particular level of understanding without any difficulty.

Telling a Story

The stories are written to give you the skeleton of a story which is complete in itself, but which can easily be adapted to suit your child better. Read the story yourself very quickly first so that you can see whether it seems basically suitable or not. Try to get your child interested in the story by changing the names of the characters and locations to those of your child's and his friends, by bringing him into the story as often as you can, and by acting yourself. All children love participating in a story. Get your child to guess what might happen next, make appropriate sound effects, invent an ending for the story and so on. Go along with your child's ideas and let him produce his own version of the story. You will find that your child expects the story to make sense and you can encourage him to interrupt if it doesn't seem to do so. Don't read the stories out flatly; bring as much expression to them as you can. If the story calls for a sneeze, your child deserves the biggest, most exaggerated sneeze you have ever made followed by the chance to make one himself. Add gestures, grimaces, face pullings and so on wherever they seem appropriate. You may feel that all this drama is simply foolish, but your audience will not. He will just be thinking what a wonderful storyteller you are and how much fun he is having, listening and joining in.

Play and Learn

The games and projects are all easy to organize quickly and don't involve you in an enormous amount of preparation. This is not only to save you time, but also because young children want to do things now, not when you have spent two hours getting them ready. The suggestions can readily be adapted and made harder or easier to suit your child's interests and abilities. The games very often give you the chance to check what your child has learned about any subject by listening to what he talks about while he plays and the instructions he gives you when you join in.

STORIES GAMES AND STUDY BOXES

Study Boxes

These have been included for those children who want more information or who seem ready to move towards the more formal exercises that they will meet in school. Do not attempt them unless your child has enjoyed all the other activities on the subject, because you will run the risk of forcing him into something he is not ready to do. Nothing is more likely to put him off doing it for ever. Although some of the exercises we have suggested look quite formal, they can easily be made enjoyable. Very many children find that learning is fun and a great deal of evidence suggests that they learn well and quickly while they enjoy it.

Drawing, modelling and writing

It's very easy to make mistakes about children's drawing and modelling. From the start, your child will want to make things, but he will not necessarily set out to produce a realistic picture or model. You should not expect him to do so. He will tell you what he is doing and the first stage in early drawing might well be called "Naming the scribble." "Here's our house," he says and you see a mess. Then you see a darker mess inside the first mess. "That's me coming out to see you," he says. If you say, "Well, it doesn't look much like a house to me", you are on the way to depriving the world of another budding artist! Let him tell you what he is drawing, encourage him, and give him new materials to try out. Finally, let him draw and model in a place where you won't spoil everything by being annoyed when you find that he has made a mess.

As your your child gets older he will want to draw you, or the cat, or an elephant. Again, he is neither skilled enough to do it realistically nor will that be what he is attempting. He will be trying to draw an elephant in the way that is right for him now. He will draw the bit which interests him biggest and he may almost forget about the rest of the picture. Don't correct this; after all, it took most of the world's artists years of study before they could realistically draw all the things that your child wants to draw right now.

Your child's approach to model-making will be very similar. At this stage, it is much more important to let him try making models in as many different materials as you can provide than to worry about whether the results realistically represent the objects he says he is modelling.

The beginnings of writing are much the same as the beginning of drawing. Scribbling leads to making more definite strokes and then to early letters, some capitals, some small, which are all sorts of sizes and shapes. Some may even be back to front or upside down. Don't worry too much about this; give him a model letter so that he gets an idea of what he is aiming for, even though his first approximations may be wide of the mark.

Praise

Finally, in all these activities don't be halfhearted about praising your child. Make sure you give him plenty of chances to succeed. When he does, or when you know that he has tried hard, give him your generous and warm praise. He will gain confidence and try to win more praise.

Exploring

Telling a Story

Auntie and the toad

Roland the toad was fed up. He had a fed up look on his face. He lived in a secret hole behind a pile of bricks in ....'s (your child's name) garden. It was a lovely, damp, dark, spidery place – the best home in the world for a toad. But now ....'s uncle had moved the bricks and Roland's home had disappeared.

........'s auntie came into the garden. She was very happy. "I've got a smart new handbag," she sang, and she put it down on the lawn while she went to smell the roses. "Oh dear," moaned Roland. "I've nowhere to go at all any more." He looked round and . . . guess what he saw? (Wait for responses.) Yes, the smart, new handbag, which was a little bit open and lovely and dark inside. So in he popped. "This might do," he mumbled. He began to explore, but it

was no good. It was dry and smelt of scent and it was clean and there were no spiders or worms to eat. There were only useless things inside it like lipstick and car keys. "This is no good to me," grumbled Roland. But before he could crawl out again, Auntie returned, picked up the bag, snapped it shut, and sang out happily, "Oh, it's such a lovely day. I'm going somewhere very special with my smart new handbag. I'm sure all the people I'm going to meet will be impressed by it."

And singing happily she trotted off with Roland squirming inside the new handbag. Well, when she arrived at her special place full of important people, you can guess what happened. She opened her handbag and . . . that's how everyone saw the new bag and Roland went exploring.

Play and Learn

Going exploring

This picture leads into the idea that we explore all around the world (as shown in later pictures in the volume). Help to start developing this idea by saying "I'm going exploring in the .... (snowy Arctic) and I'm taking .... (a sledge and lots of food and blankets) and I'm wearing .... (a thick waterproof jacket with a fur hood and thick boots, warm socks, etc). How many places can your child make good suggestions for? If she has problems give her hints ("It's a cold and snowy place," etc). If she's enjoying it, it might be worth going straight on to p.26.

Exploring at home

Do you have any dark hidy-holes around the house that your child could explore? (Built-in wardrobe, cupboards under the stairs, etc, are ideal, but check for dangers first.) Encourage her to consider what she will need in order to explore inside (a torch and notebook perhaps). Ask her questions to make her consider how different it is from outside. Does it feel different? Smell different? Sound different? It is more fun if you place some exciting things to be "discovered" there (old handbag, umbrella, magazines, etc). What can the explorer find? Encourage imaginary discoveries too.

Study Box

Safety

When children go exploring, there are a number of safety rules that you should talk through with them first. These are rules and so must be kept, although it will help to discuss the reason for making them. They are more likely to be kept if understood.

1 Always tell me where you are going. Come back to tell me if you are going somewhere else. Don't go far away. (You must agree what "far" means before they go.)
2 Try to test branches, etc, before you climb on them.
3 Anyone who is hurt must come to me. Don't ever try to bandage or cure each other.
4 Don't do anything you don't feel safe doing – even if other children are already doing it and dare you to join them.
5 Don't touch animals you don't recognize – or pets you don't know – and don't put any plants or berries in your mouth.

6 Don't go near water.
7 You may meet people you don't know. They may offer you toys, sweets, presents or a ride in a car. Say that I have told you *never* to accept. (Be careful with this; you don't want to make children frightened of strangers.)
8 Don't go off on your own.

Climbing Hills

Telling a Story

Mr Black's hill

The man next door was digging a big hole in his garden. All the earth that he dug out of the hole was piled up by the side. First it was a little pile, then a little hill and now it was a huge mountain in the back garden.

Mary and Annie watched the mountain of earth grow each day. They looked out of their bedroom window and wondered when the mountain would reach the sky. Then Mary had an idea. "Let's climb that mountain," she said to Annie. "We could get up early tomorrow morning and see who can reach the top first."

Next morning the two children woke up very early and crept out into the garden. They opened the gate next door and saw the huge mountain in front of the house. "Mr Black has been very busy digging," whispered Annie to Mary. "Look at that big hole he has made in the garden. What do you think it is for? "Never mind that," said Mary. "Let's start to climb this mountain before Mr Black gets up for work. Mary began to clamber up the mountain and Annie followed. It was hard work – they kept slipping and the earth sometimes crumbled away.

Mary was puffing and panting and was almost at the top. Suddenly her foot slipped and she fell and rolled down the pile of earth. Heaps of earth fell behind her and it kept on falling until Mr Black's hole was almost filled with earth again. Then, oh dear, Mr Black suddenly marched into his garden to see what all the noise was about. (What did Mr Black say? Was he angry? Was Mary hurt? What happened to the naughty children?)

Play and Learn

Timing climbing

Get your child to time you going up and coming down stairs, then you can time him. Try timing going up and down a ladder and so on. You can do this simply counting aloud; older children may want to use a kitchen timer or they may ask you to use your watch. If your child gets interested in the idea that going up takes longer than going down, you can carry on when you go outside together. Is there a hill near you that's steep enough to make cyclists get off and push, or that slows down buses and heavy lorries, etc?

Climbing a hill

Occasionally it's worth setting up a special climb for your child. Try stacking up some furniture, telephone directories, upturned buckets, etc. Make a summit with a flag on top and pretend it's Mount Everest. Put cushions around the base as the foothills. Tell a story of tremendous adventure, overcoming fearful odds, etc, as the climb progresses. You obviously have to make sure this activity is safe. You will probably need to be with him all the time, but the number of imaginative ideas you hear developing should make this activity a worthwhile change from more usual climbing games.

Study Box

How sand is made

At quite an early age, children begin to wonder how that beach full of sand got there. You can start them thinking in very simple terms about important weathering processes by using the stones and shells around you on the beach.

Single grains of sand are extremely hard and gritty. (This won't surprise children when they realize that they are broken down pieces of the rocks and shells on the beach.) What could be strong enough to toss these rocks and shells together and go on grinding and grinding until they are so tiny? (Wait for rough weather to explain.) What else does water do to rocks and stones? Can you find smooth, round ones? What sizes are they? Can you find a rock that water has hollowed out by swirling round and round?
(As you look for signs of wave power, you can tell your child that water breaks up rock, that it carries pebbles along with it and they get smaller and smaller as they get worn away over many, many years. Don't expect him to understand very much about this. You're really laying the foundation for lessons he will learn later.)

EXPLORING OUR WORLD
Crossing A Stream

Telling a Story

Dan and Joe's bridge

Dan and Joe went out in the country looking for blackberries one day. They crossed the little bridge over the river and soon found a bush full of huge, juicy berries. They ate some of them and they put some others in a bag. "We need a lot more to make blackberry pies," said Dan.

It was a hot and sunny afternoon and they both liked blackberry pie very much so they wandered along stopping at each bush and having a taste. They wanted the very best blackberries. Every time they thought they had enough, they saw another especially wonderful bush just a little way farther on. Then they heard the music. "It's music," said Dan. "Right out in the country," said Joe. "What can it be?"

They walked through some more bushes and there right in front of them was a wonderful sight – a fairground with lights and music and rides and stalls. "It's a fair," said Dan though he didn't need to. "Let's go."

"Er, Dan," said Joe. "Dan."

"What?" said Dan.

"It's on the other side of the river," said Joe. "We're miles away from the bridge by now."

"We could jump it," said Dan.

"Don't be silly," said Joe, "it's much too wide. What about swimming it?" But they both knew what Mum would say if they got their clothes soaked.

Then they saw an old log lying nearby and forgot about their blackberries. They started to drag the old log down to the river. "I think it's just wide enough," said Dan.

"Yes, but I'm not sure it's safe," said Joe. "Don't you think we ought to go back to the bridge?" (What do you think they did? What would you do?)

Play and Learn

Bridges and crossings

Encourage children to think about distance and length when they are playing. Help build some pillars with toy bricks, etc. Make them various distances apart and give your child pieces of card or sticks of different lengths. Let him guess which piece will bridge each gap best. Then he can go on to test if he's right. Make this very obvious for younger children and more difficult for older ones.

Stepping stones

Younger children need plenty of practice at balancing and they don't have to be very far off the floor before they find things difficult. Make a set of stepping stones out of a variety of objects, eg cushions, bits of wood, a brick, etc. Put them far enough apart to be a challenge but not too difficult. Can they cross the river? With these two games try to practise as many "distance" words as you can – "It's too long," "That's a shorter one," "Can you stretch far enough," and so on.

Study Box

Crossings
Stretch your child's imagination (and yours) by thinking up together all the different ways you could cross a stream. This can be more fun by miming the actions for each other to guess the verb – like a game of charades.

I can (jump)	across the stream	I can (paddle)	across the stream
I can (swim)	across the stream	I can (swing)	across the stream
I can (sail)	across the stream	I can (wade)	across the stream
I can (step)	across the stream	I can (fly)	across the stream

Castles

Telling a Story

Oblidob's castle

Oblidob, an old and friendly giant, was tired of living in his castle. It was too big and too cold, and too tall – even for a giant like Oblidob.

Every morning he had to climb to the very top to put up the flag. (See if your child wants to make puffing sound effects whenever you get to such a moment in the story.) And every evening he had to climb up the 1,009 steps to take it down again. (Puff, puff, puff.)

"Oh dear," he said one day. "I can't do this much more. I'm getting old. I will have to sell my castle to someone who doesn't get puffed out . . . Oh dear." And he slowly climbed up again to check the flagpole.

Now at the top of the tower lived the ravens. They had splendid nests, full of beautiful raven eggs, and they always cawed "hello" to Oblidob when he got up to the top.

One day a young giant came along. "I will buy your castle," she announced. "I am young and I don't get puffed. Just watch me!" And she ran to the very top of the stairs and all the way down again without a single huff or puff.

"Look what I found at the top," said the young giant. She showed the old giant a handful of green and brown ravens' eggs. "I just love ravens' eggs," she said, as she popped them into her mouth like sweets.

"Kaaww!" shrieked the ravens, "Kaaww! Don't sell the castle to a giant who steals birds' eggs. Keep the castle. We will fly up and put the flag out for you every morning. And we will fly up again and take it down every night. In the cold winter we will bring twigs in our beaks for your fires, and we'll caw loudly if we see an enemy."

And that's what they did, because ravens always keep to their word.

Play and Learn

A castle collection

Encourage your child to keep a special castle section in her scrapbook. Cut out pictures of castles from magazines and start a collection of postcards of castles. (Ask friends to send any cards of castles they see.) Older children may also be keen to know the names of all the different castles they come across and be given some idea of where they are. You will probably need to write these details in for them.

Castle attack

Play "knocking down the castle walls" by piling up old boxes or tins to make a fairly secure castle. Give your child a ball or a rolled-up piece of paper and see how many throws it takes to knock the castle down. While this game gives younger children good practice in throwing and aiming, older children can try to make the castle stronger (by building supports, etc). When the castle is stronger, see if they need more throws to knock it down. Can they find the weak points?

Study Box

How would you attack and defend the castle?

We have mainly emphasized the idea that castles are interesting places to visit but, of course, older children will begin to think of them as places to be attacked and defended as well.

Attack You could use machines to throw things at the walls (eg catapults, cannon). You could put ladders up and try to climb the walls. You could try to tunnel under. You could find a traitor to let you in. (You may have to explain this difficult but usually fascinating idea.)

Defences You could shut the gate (children are usually fascinated by the idea that there is only one) and stand on top of the walls and throw things down. You could send someone out at dead of night to ride off and get help, or you could rush out and attack the enemy. (Encourage your child to think of as many alternatives as possible, however bizarre they may sound.)

Keeping prisoners Most castles have dungeons, locked rooms at the top of towers and oubliettes (where prisoners were simply forgotten). This can lead to ideas about amazing escapes, etc.

MAN-MADE PLACES
Palaces

Telling a Story

The princess and the palace

Once there was a little girl who lived happily with her family and played happily with all the boys and girls who lived near her. She had lots of friends and was never lonely. But the little girl had one wish. She wanted to marry a prince and live in a palace.

Well, she was a lucky little girl and guess what happened when she grew up? Yes, she found her prince and married him. But the prince was not quite like all the princes the girl had always dreamed about. He took her back to live in his enormous palace, but it needed a lot of work. All the windows needed cleaning, everywhere needed dusting and when she went to bed, rain dripped on to her nose. "I'm afraid there are a few holes in the roof,"

said the prince. In the morning, when she woke up, she shivered and shivered. "We could never afford heating," said the prince. "I'm afraid being a prince is a very expensive business."

"We'll have to get people to come and pay to see our palace," said the girl.

"I've thought of that, but there's so much to do," said the prince, peering out at the weeds in the garden.

"Well," said the girl, "why don't you tell your soldiers to fight the weeds and polish the windows?"

"What a wonderful idea," said the prince, "and I'll make you Minister in charge of Good Ideas as well as princess, as I never have any good ideas myself."

Play and Learn

A palace game

Make your house into a palace. Invite friends to look around while your child guides them. Dress up two of the toys as a king and a queen and put them on decorated chairs that could be thrones. Develop this theme, asking your child what he would call the different rooms in your house, eg the Royal Kitchen, the Banqueting Hall, the Ballroom. Try to take him for a brief visit to see inside a palace or stately home. He will appreciate the visit after all the talk on this topic and you can buy a guide book to look through together later. This will probably give him more ideas for games at home.

Kings and queens

Kings and queens games need simple props. Don't bother making anything elaborate. Children will want to get on with the game. Cardboard, silver paper and a little glue is all you need. Once children begin to play you will hear them explore some quite important ideas. Younger children may simply enjoy the dressing-up – the finery and crowns; but older children will begin to explore their new roles and resultant powers. They may begin to issue orders, make proclamations, etc. How do they react if someone disobeys their orders? What sort of occasions warrant ceremony?

Study Box

Getting ready
Children don't always realize how many people contribute to the success of the big day. Take this idea as far as they want. Perhaps you could make up a song about it.

Groom cleans the horses; brushes their manes and tails.
Coachman polishes the coach.
Chambermaid prepares the Queen's clothes.
Lady-in-waiting chooses the Queen's jewels.
Soldiers polish their boots; iron their uniforms.

Beefeaters get their special uniforms ready.
Workmen clean the streets and put up the flags.
Policemen make sure there are no cars in the way; show the crowd where to stand; make sure the crowd don't get too close to the Queen and that people behave well.

Children make their own small flags and get ready to cheer; hope the Queen stops to talk to them. (What would they say if she did?)
Bandsmen clean their instruments and practise special tunes. Sometimes they practise near the horses to get them used to the noise.

Cathedrals

Telling a Story

Mary's visit to the cathedral

Mary couldn't see because she was blind, but that didn't stop her visiting lots of interesting places. She was especially fond of visiting very old buildings.

One day she visited Winchester Cathedral in England and met the man in charge of the whole cathedral. He was called a Bishop. The Bishop told Mary that the cathedral was 900 years old.

It was very quiet in the cathedral and there was a nice but unusual smell. The Bishop explained that cathedrals often have a "musty" smell because the stone walls are so old and sometimes a little bit damp. He also told Mary that Winchester Cathedral almost fell down a hundred years ago because it was sinking into the ground. A brave man had spent all his life working underneath it with cement in order to stop such a terrible thing happening.

"That's good," said Mary. "I wouldn't want such a wonderful building as this to fall down." Just as she said these words the Bishop knocked into a huge stand with candles on it. Crash! went the iron stand. Bang! went a heavy wooden chair beside it. The sounds echoed round the cathedral ... The Bishop gave a little laugh. "Oh dear," he said, "I am so clumsy today. I dropped my egg at breakfast, and now I've knocked a chair and candlestand over." Mary laughed, "You ought to learn to move round as carefully as I can – or you will knock the whole cathedral over one day, and I wouldn't like that!"

Play and Learn

Silence and sounds

Ask your child what sounds she thinks she would hear in a cathedral. Would it be quiet? How would people talk to each other? (Very quietly, maybe in whispers.) Can she whisper? Explain that places of worship are normally quiet so that people can think and worship without distractions. See if you can get her to be completely quiet for a minute (she won't manage much longer) then ask what sounds she heard. She may hear all sorts of perfectly normal sounds that she does not usually notice: dripping taps, water going through pipes, creaking floorboards and other sounds that houses make.

Making a guide book

Point out the boy using a guide book in the picture. Explain to your child that guide books tell people all about the interesting things they should see when visiting a particular building. See if she'd like to help you make a guide book of your home. Let your child cut or tear pictures of rooms out of old magazines and then stick them into a simple book. You could make the book by folding some pieces of newsprint or wrapping-paper in half and then sewing them down the middle. Let your child guide visitors around your home and show them all the sights and treasures in it.

Study Box

In a cathedral
Cathedrals are places of worship (like mosques, synagogues and temples) and children may well want to know what happens in them. It's worth pointing out that many religions worship in similar ways although their beliefs are different.

Prayers Every day (morning, afternoon and evening) prayers are said to thank God for things and also, sometimes, to ask for things.
Hymns People love singing in cathedrals. There is always an organ, a choir and special songs (but note that mosques do not have music).

Help People go to see priests in cathedrals if they need help. The priests always try to advise them.
Reading Most religions have an important book: The Bible (Christianity), The Koran (Islam), The Talmud (Judaism), The Bhagavad Gita and others (Hinduism).

Extracts are usually read aloud by the priest as part of the service.
Getting married Sometimes important or famous people get married in cathedrals.
Meeting place People often only see each other when they go to the cathedral, so it can act as a meeting place too.

MAN-MADE PLACES
Bridges

Telling a Story

The red-headed seagull

Bert the bridge painter was hard at work painting the harbour bridge a fine bright red. Just then a seagull flew by. "Watch it!" said Bert. "He's going for your food."

"Just my luck," said Alf, as the seagull snatched up a pack of bread and cheese. Bert was quicker. He picked up a huge pot of paint and threw it at the seagull. "Now you've done it," said Alf. "I knew you'd make a mess."

They watched as the pot fell through the sky turning over and over until it fell neatly straight down a ship's funnel. There was a moment's quiet and then the ship shivered and shuddered and a huge puff of red paint came shooting up all over the bridge. "Hooray!" yelled Bert. "We've done it! The whole bridge in one day!" But far below they could see a bright red motorcyclist and a bright red sportscar. "Maybe it would be a good idea to stay up here for a while," said Bert. "The ship doesn't seem to be very good at getting the paint in the right place."

"Well, you'll have to share your lunch with me if we do," said Alf. "I'm starving."

"OK," said Bert. "It's meat pie today."

"It would be if you hadn't gone and dropped it in the paint," said Alf, as he held a bright red meat pie above his head. It shone in the sun.

"Caw!" said the seagull and he snatched it away.

"That's funny," said an excited bird watcher on the bridge. "I've never seen a red-headed seagull before. Perhaps it's a new kind of bird."

But we know what it was, don't we?

Play and Learn

Bridge play

Simple bridges can help to develop several physical skills. Make a bridge together out of chairs and boxes and a plank of wood. See how many different ways your child can think to get over it and under it. If he can't get under it then see if he can adapt it so that he can be sure that he really is using his body as well as he might. Then ask him whether he thinks it safe for him to cross it. Has he checked its strength? Does it need more supports underneath? If he is hesitant to try, hold his hand and help him. If he is still reluctant then don't force the issue.

Building bridges

Build a simple bridge together over a bowl of water, using something like a ruler. Let your child test his aim by seeing if he can run a car from one end to the other without it falling in the water. Let your child construct different kinds of bridges using pieces of card, bricks or other similar material. Test each bridge for strength by seeing whether it can carry a number of toy cars and if it will carry toy trucks loaded with weights. Does the bridge need more support at either end? He will soon realize what disasters can happen if a bridge is not constructed carefully.

Study Box

All kinds of bridges
It's worth taking time to look quite carefully at bridges because children often enjoy them. Don't go into too much technical detail, just look around near home and on journeys for interesting ones.

Suspension bridge This is the bridge in the picture. The roadway is suspended from the wire cables, which go over the supporting pillars and are firmly anchored at each end of the bridge.
Lifting bridge Two halves of the bridge lift up. They are often found near docks where building space is limited.
Swing bridge The whole bridge swings to one side.
Flyovers Carry traffic across other roads.
Pedestrian or animal bridges Not for traffic. Often go over motorways.
Humpback bridges Often found in country areas.

Drawbridge Security bridge (sometimes used by castles with moats) that can be lowered for someone to cross or raised back into the wall for defence.
Timber-framed bridge Old wooden bridge with huge supports. Often cross gorges, canyons, etc.

Modern Buildings

Telling a Story

Noisy Sydney Opera-House

It was very, very late at night and there was singing coming from Sydney Opera-House, "Whooo hoo taa laa." He loved being lit up at night and singing loudly. But the yachts and boats tied up on the river were not happy at all.

"Listen to us!" they cried. "We've been busy working all day on the river giving people rides, and now that it is night and we want to sleep you are keeping us all awake!"

Next day the boats all had a meeting. They were all yawning. Can you guess why? "Yaawaaan," said the yacht with the red sails. "We must do something, or we will get so tired that we won't be able to float."

"But there's nothing we can do," yawned Blue Sail.

"Oh yes, there is," laughed the three big river boats. "Just listen to this: BAA! HOOOOOOOTTAAAA! WHAAAHOOT"

went their mighty hooters. (Repeat, with your child helping.) "Opera-House has been singing all night, and in the day he snoozes." Suddenly they heard Sydney bellow out, "Keep quiet you noisy river boats, I can't have my morning snooze with that dreadful hooting."

"But you sing when we are trying to sleep," shouted the boats all together. "It's the same for us at night."

So they had a meeting and Sydney said he wouldn't sing so late, and that he would sing a little more quietly, and that he would shut his windows. That made the boats happy. "OK," they said, "we will hoot for one last time and then we won't disturb you ever again. One – two – three –" Sydney put his fingers in his ears and decided he'd better keep his promise. And, so far as I know, he has.

Play and Learn

Who am I?

Opera singers perform in such buildings as Sydney Opera House. Football and baseball players play in stadiums. Play a game with your child where you describe a (special) building in which someone works and she has to guess who you are. "I go to work up lots and lots of steps, hundreds and hundreds, in a very tall building that looks out to sea. At the top I find a bright light." (A lighthouse keeper.) Describe places children already know, eg supermarket, farm, pet shop, fire station, library, etc. Let your child ask you questions too.

Skyscrapers

Let your child make a magnificent skyscraper from household objects. Supply her with any old cereal or detergent packets, dried milk tins, boxes, books, cotton reels, etc. (The more variety the better.) Encourage her to make the tallest and prettiest skyscraper ever. Be ready to give assistance if it is needed. Once your child feels confident about constructing the building, see how she feels about the design. Do the colours of the packets go well together? How different do they look when arranged another way? Don't do this kind of work on a carpet. It doesn't provide a firm enough base.

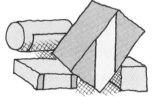

Study Box

Making the Opera House
Children don't often appreciate architecture in the way adults do, but they can get to learn that a large number of people are involved in making buildings. Ask who they think helped to make this one and see if they know what all the people do.

Architect planned building. Chose place to build it where it would look best. Worked out how to build curving shapes. (Could your child build curves with blocks? She won't be able to, but may appreciate how difficult it is.)
Surveyors worked out how much cement they would need

to build the opera house. (You could point out that they would have to be very good at sums to do this.)
Excavators dug out holes for foundations.
Cement mixers made tons and tons of cement.
Builders put it in the right place and built everything: the

walls, the roof and everything inside.
Electricians, Carpenters, Painters, etc, put in the lights and the wires and decorated everything. And finally don't forget the people of Australia, who paid for it!

LANDMARKS
Rain And Rivers

Telling a Story

Mr Bingo's trip

This is a story about something big and fat and red that floats in the sky. Guess what? That's right – it's a big balloon that people can ride in, and the balloon's name is Tubby. Well, Tubby belonged to a man called Mr Bingo. On sunny days Mr Bingo would climb into Tubby's big basket and fly as high as the clouds.

One day Mr Bingo was up in Tubby when he noticed some children at a school all playing together in the play-ground. Very slowly he steered Tubby right down into the playground. All the children climbed into the basket. They all knew Mr Bingo and their teacher said they could go with him. Then up Tubby flew. Off they went up into the sky. They were getting closer and closer to the clouds, but they never seemed to quite reach them.

"Oh look!" cried Maggie Jones. "Look at the little water-mill!"

"Oooh, look!" shrieked Bobby. "I can see people in sailing boats." "Oh look! I can see ...." (And so on. Use all the other events in the picture.)

Suddenly Tubby was blown sideways by the wind. "Whoops!" cried Mr Bingo, and he spilt his glass of orange drink right over the edge of the basket. "Oh dear!" cried everyone as they saw all the orange drink spilling down through the sky.

Far, far below the children could see Mr Brown coming out for his afternoon walk. Suddenly, he darted back indoors and came out with an umbrella. "He must think it's raining orange drink. Well done Tubby, you've given Mr Brown a nice surprise," laughed the children. (If your child likes this story you can easily make up other adventures for Tubby and Mr Bingo.)

Play and Learn

Running water

Children are fascinated by the way water flows. They can learn a lot if you are able to arrange simple outdoor activi-ties for them. Put a hose on, or let them use a watering can or jug to watch how water makes a path for itself. Does it spread all over the place or make a channel? Can they stop the water's flow? What happens when they do? What does the water carry along with it?

Making a rainbow

After painting rainbows, try dressing in rainbow colours. Can your child put on a piece of clothing for each colour (eg a red hat, orange scarf, yellow sweater, green belt, etc)? If there are several children available each one can try and dress in a rain-bow-coloured piece of clothing. Then see if they can sort themselves out to stand in rainbow colour order (they'll probably need reminding with some rain-bow pictures). Try and let them look in a mirror so they see the whole rainbow.

Study Box

Weather words
Ask children what different weather words mean to them. Say the word first and ask your child to describe it. Most children will want to work with you to fill in the chart, but the ones who enjoy this may want you to give them more words.

It will be	Sun	Frost	Thunder	Rain
Hot	√			
Cold				
Wet				
Dry	√			

Islands

Telling a Story

A letter from Nicos

Nicos lived on an island in Greece. One day his mother told him that his cousin Andreas was coming to stay. Andreas lived in Athens, the biggest city in Greece. Nicos' mother thought that he'd find life on their island very different. So she suggested to Nicos that he should write a letter to his cousin to tell him about their life. This is what Nicos wrote:

"Dear Andreas,
I am looking forward to your visit next month. My mother and I will come to meet you at the harbour and take you home. We live in a farmhouse outside the village. We have a lot of different animals: goats, sheep and chickens. Most of them help to give us food, but the donkey, Pino, is useful for carrying things.

"When I am not at school I help on the farm or go to the market. One day I was taking some fruit down to the shops to sell. Pino's baskets were piled high. I felt very sleepy and sat down under a tree to rest. I fell asleep, but when I woke up, Pino had gone. I rushed down to the shops and there was Pino standing in the shade of a tree! I was so happy. Even though he is rather slow, he is very clever and knows his way around most of the island.

In the summer my mother works at a hotel as well as on the farm. But in the winter there aren't many visitors. When I grow up I want to be a fisherman. I often go down to the harbour and talk to the men mending their nets.

"One of my favourite games is throwing stones. I am the third best of all the children I know. One day I want to be able to throw a stone farther than anyone else.

"Well, that's all I will tell you about today. See you soon. Nicos."
What do you think Andreas wrote back?

Play and Learn

I spy

The amount of detail in this picture makes it a very good one to play "I spy" with. Give clues such as "I spy something which is alive and white and gives us some material for clothes" (sheep), and "I spy something that is fast and red" (speedboat). Encourage your child to put questions such as "Is it a boat?" rather than to merely guess the answer (eg "It's the speedboat").

Island game
Children quite often make islands for themselves when they are in the bath or paddling pool. Even though all they have done is bend their knee, they still love the idea that it's completely surrounded by water. A few obvious toys can help them start making journeys to and from the island and suggestions from you will soon get them carrying different cargoes to and fro and generally developing the ideas they have had while working with you on this picture.

Study Box

How we live
This picture could be a useful starting point for drawing comparisons between different life-styles. The differences will be especially marked if you live in a large town or city; but wherever you live, stress the fact that people everywhere have to do similar things.

Common needs	How islanders get them
Food	Farming, fishing, shopping (Little choice on island)
Water	Taps or wells (No reservoir on island)
Housing	Local materials (Type may depend on climate)
Clothes	May make their own (No clothes shops on island)
Transport	Difficult to get petrol or large vehicles to island
Leisure	Hire films, organize own dances, parties

Jungles

Telling a Story

Jenny's jungle

One day Jenny was looking in a picture book and she saw a place that looked very different from where she lived: no houses and roads, no people to be seen. It looked as if it would be very quiet there.

"I wish I could go to this place," thought Jenny as she curled up on the big sofa. She began to dream.

She was in a really noisy place, birds screeched and monkeys chattered and insects chirped and whined and buzzed. Jenny felt excited as she looked at the hundreds of new things. "I'm the first person to be here and see all this," she said proudly.

"What about me? What about me?" she heard all around her. It was the birds and creatures who lived there. "You don't count," she said. "You are not people."

"Ah, but we often see people go through here."

The creatures showed Jenny what they knew: which plants to eat, where to find drinking water and, at last, they took her to a secret village.

The people showed Jenny their houses, which were made from the trees and creepers of the forest. They painted patterns on Jenny's skin and made her a basket to gather fruit and berries to eat. Then Jenny went to sleep, safe from the rain in a house made of wood and leaves. But when she woke up, she was back on the sofa at home and her picture book was lying on the floor.

"Have you been hiding?" asked her mother. But Jenny smiled and said not a word, in case her mother didn't believe that she had been to the jungle and back!

Play and Learn

Exploring

Make a jungle using furniture (eg table and chair legs with cushions stuck between them and old clothes draped around). See how many ways your child can find to get through all the obstacles, under and over the chairs, through the armrests, etc. Help her become aware of what she is doing by asking questions: "Where do you get stuck? Is it fun? Do you sometimes think you are stuck and will never get out, and then you think of a way?" Older children can try moving through the jungle without touching the floor.

Snake play

Stuff an old sock or stocking with cloth or paper and tie up the end with string. Draw or stick eyes on the snake and tie a long piece of string or cotton to its neck. Hold on to this while you hide the snake under a chair or rug supported by books or small boxes. Let your child creep up to the snake's den to touch its head. Just as she is about to grab it, jerk the string – now the snake is the hunter. There will be lots of shrieking and excitement and you won't need to make things any more complicated. Remember to reverse the roles and let your child have a turn with the hunting snake.

Study Box

Exploring in the jungle
Look again at the people unloading the boat and ask what the luggage would be. Encourage your child to realize that the explorers need equipment for different purposes when they are on a field trip.

For living	For working	For reporting
Tents	Butterfly nets	Movie camera
Cooking pots	Field glasses	Tape recorder
Sleeping bags	Magnifying glass	Pencils and paints
Rainwear	Tins for keeping plants	Notebooks
Food	Measuring instruments	Ordinary camera
First-aid kit	Canvas bags for snakes	Radio

Mountain Tops

Telling a Story

Up the hill and back again

Peter and Val and Rags and Dad got turned out of the house one afternoon. "Off you go, you lot," said Mum. "I'm busy, you go off for a walk."

"Where shall we go?" asked Dad.

"Let's go up to the top of the big hill," said Val.

"We'll never get all the way up there," Peter gasped. "It's not a hill, it's a great mountain." But they started off all the same. Soon they were puffing and panting as they struggled up the steep hill. Rags raced by waving his tail. "It's not fair," said Peter. "He's got four legs and we've only got two. He might at least give us a pull."

"Save your breath," said Dad. "You'll need it all."

All of a sudden they were at the top. "There," said Val. "I told you we could do it. We're really good mountain climbers. There's our house with the car outside."

"That's not our house," said Peter. "It's much too little and that's only a toy car. Look at the toy lady putting a bucket down beside the car."

"That's not a toy lady," said Dad. "That's Mum."

"I don't believe you," said Peter. "Our mum's much bigger than that."

"Come on, I'll show you," said Val. "Race you down." They went dashing off down the hill.

When the children arrived Mum had finished washing the car. "There," said Val, "I said it was Mum. Now look." And she turned Peter round and pointed to the hill. "Coo," he said, "did we go all the way up there? Look at those funny little people walking up there now."

Play and Learn

Pouring water

Children learn to pour water long before they understand any of the principles involved. You can gradually introduce important ideas to them, such as the simple fact that water always runs downhill. Get your child to sit in the bath with his knees up. Play pouring water from different things – a cup, his hand, a sponge – on to his knee. Which way does it run? Can he make it run upwards? Of course he can't, but that doesn't mean he shouldn't try! Trying to do impossible things is a useful way of learning so long as you don't force him to try for too long.

What can you see?

Put his favourite toy on the floor. Tell your child to go to different parts of the room and look at it. Give directions, eg "Take two steps backwards and look at it. Turn round, open your legs, bend over and look at it through your legs." Does it look the same each time or does it look different? If there are several children, tell them to sit round the room in different places and each describe exactly what they can see. They will soon realize that the child who is in front of the toy can see bits of it which the one behind it can't see. They may start being able to guess what someone else can see.

Study Box

How do mountaineers climb?

Even if you do not know very much about climbing yourself, there are some fairly basic ideas you can tell your child.

Mountaineers climb as a team. The leader works out the route and finds the best places to put hands and feet. If it's icy, he cuts out steps with his axe. In difficult places, he sometimes drives a big nail (a piton) into the rock so that he can stand on it. The second man is the anchor man. He holds the rope and often puts it round a rock so that he can hold tight if the leader falls. The leader sets off up a stretch of rock and the anchor man waits until he is safely up. Then the leader guides the anchor man up and starts climbing again. When mountaineers climb very high mountains they often pitch tents on tiny ledges and sleep hanging in mid-air!

Older children often enjoy rock climbing and you shouldn't stop them, but make sure the rocks they are on are safe and that they don't climb immediately under each other, as there's danger from falling stones.

LANDMARKS

Deep Caves

 Telling a Story

Discovering a cave

Right in the middle of the holiday, Claire's dad said, "What does the word *cave* make you think of?"

"Treasure," said Louise.

"Monsters," said Matthew.

"Deep, dark, wet," said Claire, who was a little bit scared of caves.

"Well," said Dad, "I've found one for us to visit. Let's go and see what we can find."

And they all went off in the car to a special cave that was near their campsite. When they got there, Dad paid for the tickets and they all went into the dark entrance.

"Let's pretend we're the first people ever to come here," said Louise. They all went carefully down the steps looking at the dark rocks. Claire held Dad's hand, but Matthew

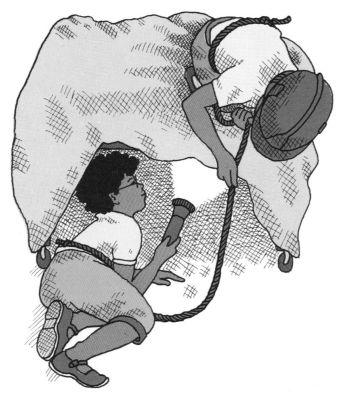

and Louise went on front. They turned a corner and stopped dead in their tracks.

The walls of the room were covered with wonderful paintings. They were of animals and people and birds. The children stared at them.

"Whoever made those?" asked Claire. "They don't look like the kind of drawings we make today."

"No they are not," said Dad. "They were made thousands of years ago by the first people who ever came here."

"Oh dear," said Matthew, "I was pretending to be the first person to come down here but I never thought it was that long ago."

"No," said Louise, "but they are lovely pictures. Let's find out about the people who painted them."

Play and Learn

Cave play

Many children will find it hard to realize that there is no natural light in a deep cave and very few sounds. It's obviously not safe for them to go near caves by themselves, but you could create one at home by drawing curtains to make a room completely dark. Leave a door open with an outside light for children who might be frightened and encourage them to imagine that they are going into an unexplored cave full of stalactites and stalagmites. You should hear them describing all the sights and sounds they come across as they get more involved in the game.

Going caving

Underneath the bed there is a mysterious land that children love exploring. It's usually not difficult to make it fairly dark and you can arrange a few surprise items if you have time (a mirror and some silver paper hanging up to represent stalactites are enough). Then dress children up as potholers (with hard hats for protection), rope them together and give one of them a small torch. If you darken the whole room, they can come in and explore round it. Suddenly they discover the new cave . . . Let them get fairly familiar with the darkened room before they go under the bed.

Study Box

How caves are made

Older children may well ask you to explain some of the facts about caves and you can start to give them a few simple ideas, even though experts do not completely agree about some of the details.

Most **inland caves** are formed in country where the underlying rock is limestone. Rainwater can gradually soften the limestone and wash it away. The rain sinks holes in the rock and streams begin to pour down the resulting "chimneys". Underground streams wash through long galleries and tunnels.

Stalactites and stalagmites are formed as the water drips slowly through cracks in the rock. The water in each drop evaporates, but a tiny quantity of minerals is left behind, sticking to the rock. Each drip adds a little more minerals. All this happens very slowly – some stalactites grow 2.5cm (1in) every 4,000 years!

Caves in sea cliffs are often made by the sea finding a weakness in the rock and washing it away.

There is a picture about early cave-dwellers and cave paintings on p.46 of the volume IN THE PAST.

The Sea Bed

Telling a Story

■■■■ and the people

■■■■ the pink-spotted crab lived with her auntie under a ■■■■ cannon right inside an old and very rotten galleon. ■■■■ crabs always think a lot and one day when she was thinking, Pansy said to her aunt, who was called Maud, "Aunt Maud, who lives up there?" and she pointed towards the sky, which glimmered dimly above them.

"Oh people live up there," said Aunt Maud. "They live in things called ships."

"Oh," said Pansy, and thought again. "What are people like who live up there in ships?"

"Oh, they are very funny things," said Aunt Maud, "very funny things, people are. They've only got two legs and they don't even have proper claws."

"I'd love to see a people," thought Pansy. Just then she noticed Aunt Maud had dozed off, so she decided to take a peep outside the galleon. She wriggled out and looked up and there was a SPLASH and lots of bubbles. Pansy hid behind a large rock. Suddenly she saw what had made the big splash. Guess what it was? Yes, it was a people!

Pansy took one look and scuttled back into the galleon. "Auntie, Auntie!" she cried, shivering with fear, "I've seen one. I've seen a PEOPLE. They are horrible. They have a great big glass face, huge black webbed feet, a big lump on their backs and they blow fizzing bubbles all the time."

"Yes, I know," said Aunt Maud, slowly chewing a piece of dead winkle. "I know. They are very, very strange things. People are the funniest looking things in the whole wide world."

Play and Learn

Underwater acting

Begin a game by acting occupations that are in the Study Box. The children guess what you are pretending to be by calling out the correct single word: ie "Diver" and not "The man swimming along with flippers." Go on to mime the fish after you have done Diver. If the calling out interrupts the acting too much, it is a good idea to insist that no guesses are made until the act is completed. Then let your child have a turn at acting while you guess. Encourage him to think out what he's going to do carefully before he starts: children may rush into their acts and then get stuck.

Treasure hunt

Wrap a variety of ordinary objects up in bags choosing some that are very common and one or two that are quite special. Wrap them very roughly, so your child can't tell what's inside. Tie string on to each bundle and put them in a deep box, dustbin, etc. Tell a short story about the sunken treasure ship and the divers who discovered it. Then go off to haul the treasure up, unwrap it and admire it. If you can make some of the bags different weights, your child will have more fun guessing the contents as each object comes to the surface. This kind of activity can be adapted for parties.

Study Box

Names	Description	Job	
Children need help in realizing that we can often use one word to describe someone and his occupation. They tend to start by describing the whole action.	The person who swims down to the bottom of the sea	is called a diver	*The idea of introducing one word for varied occupations is an interesting and useful activity, but try to select occupations that your children already know. They can't work in this way if you make it too difficult for them.*
	The people who were on the ship which sank	would have been called sailors	
	People who take pictures of fish, or us, or anything	are called photographers	

CELEBRATIONS
Greek Wedding

Telling a Story

The bridesmaid's spots

One day Sharon, who was six, had some wonderful news. She was going to be a bridesmaid. Her big sister, Jeanette, was going to marry Michael. They were going to be married at .... (choose somewhere in your child's area). Jeanette was going to wear a beautiful white dress. Michael was going to wear a brown suit, and they bought Sharon a silky dress with frills as pretty as a butterfly.

"The wedding is next week," explained Jeanette, "and I want you to keep yourself clean and tidy for the special day. You will walk behind me down the aisle at church and carry flowers for me. I hope you will walk beautifully and behave yourself."

On the evening before the wedding Sharon had a bath and went into the bedroom where Jeanette was trying on her dress. "Now you be good tomorrow, Sharon," said Jeanette. "Don't trip over my dress. Don't laugh in the service. Don't eat too much." The don'ts went on and on. Just before bedtime Jeanette even said, "Don't catch chicken-pox in the night will you?"

Next morning, when Sharon's mother went to wake her up she had a terrible surprise!

"Oh no! Jeanette come quickly. Look what's happened to Sharon in the night!" Her face was covered with red spots. Millions of them!

"Oh dear!" cried Jeanette. And then Sharon burst out laughing and Sharon's mother and poor Jeanette looked at the stick of old lipstick on the dressing table and realized naughty Sharon had tricked them both!

Play and Learn

Happy families

Not surprisingly, children don't always understand exactly what each partner is promising at a wedding and how their lives will change. Simple games such as this one, which reminds them that the partners will usually share the same name, can help: When people get married they are usually called Mr and Mrs. Can your child think of good names for them? (Mr and Mrs Crumb the bakers, Mr and Mrs Rose the gardeners, etc.) You can go further with older children by asking for an address: Mr and Mrs Crumb the bakers live in Loaf Street, Doughtown, etc.

Paper money game

Make some paper money together by cutting newspaper into note-shaped pieces. You will need quite a lot of it. Then remind your children about the custom of sticking money on the bride and groom's clothes and suggest they see how much money they can attach to each other without using pins. Each note must be visible, no stuffing it in pockets. After a while, see who has most, who has found the cleverest way to put it on, etc. Younger children will simply enjoy this stage of the game; older children can go on to say how they will use the money in their new home.

Study Box

Wedding customs
Here are a few customs from different parts of the world for children who are interested in them. Do they know what their own customs symbolize?

Germany The bride's veil is torn up and unmarried girls try to get a piece. The bridegroom's mother throws rice over bride; the grains which stick to her show how many children she will have.
Bedouin Bride seated on camel is led seven times round tent, which she then enters.

Hindu Roasted grain is thrown on a fire as offering to gods. The groom leads his bride round the fire. Bride and groom take seven solemn steps together.
China Pomegranates are usually given as gifts. They express the hope that the couple will have children.

Rings Given all over the world as a sign of eternity because they have no end and no beginning. Often placed on third finger because people used to believe that a nerve ran straight to the heart from it.

A Japanese Ceremony

Telling a Story

Sachiko's day

Sachiko lived in Japan. She was three years old. Being three is always important, but in Japan this is a very special birthday. Soon there would be the celebration of Shichi-Go-San when children who are three, five and seven are taken by their mums and dads to a shrine to say "thank you" for growing up to be healthy and strong.

But Sachiko did not have a mum, and her dad was living far away because of his work. Sachiko would go to the shrine with her aunt, whom she lived with and loved very much. Sachiko felt sad, though, when she knew her friends would have mums and dads with them at the celebrations. "I don't think Shichi-Go-San day will be quite so special for me," she whispered to the birds when she was in her garden at home.

Now sometimes in gardens magic things happen and this day there was magic in the air. The birds understood what Sachiko was talking about. They told the flowers and the sun about Sachiko's sadness. One little bird even went to Sachiko's aunt to tell her the problem.

When the day arrived, the sun shone brightly. The flowers and trees looked beautiful. The birds sang a special song for her. Sachiko felt the sun, looked at the flowers and listened to the birds. "It really is a special day," she said. Then, just as it was time to go to the shrine, there was a knock at the door. Sachiko ran to answer it. There on the doorstep was a man with a big smile. Sachiko squealed with delight and leapt into his arms. Guess who it was. How do you think he had found out?

Play and Learn

Strange celebrations

No doubt your child thinks some of the celebrations in this section are very strange and so it's a good idea to help him realize that, although people celebrate different festivals in different ways, the feelings involved are often very much the same. Let him choose a family celebration he knows. Pretend you are a complete stranger from another country. Can he explain it to you? Pretend enormous disbelief: "They hang up their socks? At the end of the bed? I don't believe it; what on earth do they do that for? For presents? Whoever would put presents in a sock?" Etc.

Making a shrine

Decorate a sheet of card with objects your child has collected – coins, bottle tops, a ribbon, foil paper, etc. Put a small candle safely in front at the base. Darken the room and sit as close as you safely can. Once you have both enjoyed the splendour and peace of this miniature shrine, see if your child is interested in making it a shrine for his toys. He could dress them up in special clothes and let them take part in a ritual. Can your child make up a story with you to say what they are all doing and why? Can he think of some things that he would like to give thanks for at his shrine?

Study Box

Our family

Children don't find it easy to sort relationships out, but they do find them fascinating and they often think it's very important to know who is who. Older children will enjoy trying to sort out quite complicated relationships.

Joe is Mary's **brother**	Mary is his **sister**	Tom is Joe's **dad**	Joe is his **son**
Ann is Mary's **mum**	Mary is her **daughter**	Tom is Mary's **dad**	Mary is his **daughter**
Ann's **sister** is called Margaret	Margaret is Mary and Joe's **aunt**	Ann is married to Tom	She is his **wife**, he is her **husband**
Ann's **brother** is called Jim	Jim is Mary and Joe's **uncle**	Jim has two children	They are Mary and Joe's **cousins**

CELEBRATIONS
A Folk Dance

Telling a Story

A dance for Grant

One day last summer Paul's mother went into hospital to have a baby. She was away a whole week and Paul was feeling a little bit sad. He had not got any brothers and sisters and he was being looked after by Mrs Grant, who lived next door.

Mrs Grant came to Paul's country from Africa and she had five children of her own. One day there was a telephone call to Mrs Grant from the hospital.

"Your mummy and baby brother are coming home after dinner," she told Paul. "Won't that be lovely? In my village, when I was living in Africa as a little girl," Mrs Grant went on, "we used to make up a dance and a song to say thank you for mummies and babies. Why don't you make one up for your mum and new baby brother?"

At three o'clock an ambulance drew up and out walked Paul's mother with a white bundle in her arms. As she walked up the steps six people waving sticks with brightly coloured paper streaming merrily from the ends appeared. They were dressed in old dressing gowns, masks and Mrs Grant's old hats. And they sang:
"Paul's got a baby, Paul's got a baby.
Now there's two, now there's two.
Whooo Hooo Hoo."

And when they did the "Whooo Hooo Hoo" part they all jumped high in the air and even did cartwheels.

"What a lovely welcome home," sighed Paul's mother. "I think I'll call him after you all." She squeezed Paul's hand and said, "Shall we call him Grant?"

Play and Learn

Rhythm

Games that help develop your child's sense of rhythm are very valuable in developing both musical and listening skills. Suggest children could clap like the people in the picture, and start a very simple rhythmic dance going. Choose two or three children to be "clappers" with you and let the others be dancers. Change clappers and dancers round so everyone has a turn at each, or clap while your child dances if you are alone together. Of course the dance needs to be for something – a birthday, etc. Don't vary the rhythm much until your child understands what to do.

Drumming

Most children love drumming and will drum away until you call a halt. As soon as older children begin to enjoy clapping games, and play them properly, you can start using the drum (or a tambourine) more purposefully. Tap out a very simple rhythm for your child to march to. At this stage, you will be tempted to make the beat more complicated or to introduce a variety of instruments before your child has really mastered keeping in time with the beat. Resist the temptation as it's all too easy to cause confusion rather than the feeling of togetherness which is so important in music.

Study Box

Dances
The origins of most folk dances stretch right back to pre-Christian and earlier times. Although the dances are mostly performed for fun today, the movements still have meaning. Here are a few ideas for other dances.

Devil dances are performed in Kandy, Sri Lanka, by dancers wearing red cloths on their heads. They bring good fortune to persons afflicted by disease, insanity or bad luck.
Initiation dances 8–12-year-old Panare children from South America dance together before going out into the forest alone for the first time. They are not considered adult until they can hunt, fish and make a forest clearing. (Children could invent actions for this.)
War dances On Papua New Guinea islands, whole tribes take part in war dances. When missionaries taught the islanders to play cricket, they incorporated dance actions in the game and now perform ritual dances before their matches, which the home team always wins.
Animal dances take place all over the world. They are often associated with hunting or fertility, with dancers dressed as animals.

Midsummer Festival

Telling a Story

Inga's garland

Inga lived in a village in Sweden. In the winter it was cold and dark when Inga went to school, but now the summer had arrived. Everyone was very happy to see the sun again and soon people began talking about the Midsummer Festival to be held in the village.

All the children in Inga's school were excited. This year their teachers told them that there would be a competition for growing the prettiest flowers. The winner would have her flowers placed on top of the big pole which always decorated the village for the festival. But Inga felt sad; her friends were busy growing beautiful flowers in their large gardens, but Inga did not have a garden in her flat. She did grow little plants in pots by the window, but there weren't enough of them to make a big bunch.

The day before the competition Inga was walking home from school through the woods. She was looking at some of the wild flowers when she saw a small budgerigar lying on the ground looking very cold and hungry. She picked it up and saw that it had a tiny plastic ring with writing on it on its leg. "Hans Johannsen, Florist, Main Street," she read.

Inga went along the main street till she found Mr Johannsen's shop. There it was, full of beautiful garlands of flowers ready for tomorrow. You should have seen Mr Johannsen's face when Inga walked in. He was so pleased – it was his best budgie. He was so grateful that he gave her the most beautiful garland in the shop. Inga didn't win the competition, but she did have the loveliest garland.

Play and Learn

Having a celebration

Start celebrations at home by getting your child to think of a good reason for celebrating (a new baby or pet animal in the house, a sunny day, a wet day after a dry spell, visitors to stay – virtually anything can give cause for celebration). Then ask what special things can be made for this celebration? Suggest making a garland, wearing national dress, making a special meal, but also see if you can encourage original ideas or better ways of improving on a traditional custom. If possible, arrange to share the celebration with a visitor.

A summer dance

Children enjoy using flowers and other natural materials to make simple chains and garlands, and you can point out that summer is the best time of year for doing this. When they start to want to dance, they are likely to want you to join in with them. Give their dancing a little direction by giving them something to use as a maypole, and encourage them to work out what they are celebrating. Suggest a few different kinds of steps – slow and solemn lifting your feet up high, quick and light, etc – and then leave them to develop the dance and join the steps together.

Study Box

Festivals
Many countries celebrate very similar events even though they may do so at different times of year. How would your children celebrate these events? What songs would they sing? What dances would there be?

Time of year	Festival	Special features
Winter	Christmas	Crackers, special foods, etc
Winter or spring	New Year	Making resolutions
Spring	Things growing	Maypoles, dancing, flowers
Autumn	Harvest	Piles of crops

CELEBRATIONS
Carnival

Telling a Story

The costume competition

Today was the day Steve had been waiting for all year. He and his friends and their teachers at school had been working hard making their bird costumes for today's competitions. They talked and thought of little else: each of them dreamed of winning the competition.

Steve felt nearly sick with excitement as he got ready. He thought the birds' feathers and costumes were the most splendid anyone could imagine. But when he saw the other groups' costumes he was shocked. They all had magnificent outfits as well. They were dressed as flowers and space invaders and even people who had come from a country under the sea. In fact he was no longer sure that his school's were the best. He felt disappointed that after so much hard work, he and his friends mightn't win the competition after all.

His elder sister came up and asked him why he looked so sad. When he explained, she told him to stop being silly. Of course everyone dreamed of winning competitions, but the main thing about Carnival was to enjoy yourself. You certainly wouldn't win any competitions just looking fed up. So Steve tried to cheer up. He started to jump along to the music. He even began to feel happy.

In the end, he and the rest of his school group came second in the competition. The space invaders won with their glittering costumes. It wasn't what he dreamed of, but it was still by far the best day of the year. Steve made up his mind to start planning for next year straight away. (What do you think he decided to be?)

Play and Learn

Rhythmic games

As soon as your child shows that he is beginning to be able to make simple clapping rhythms, you can move on to playing along with music. A saucepan and wooden spoon make an excellent drum, a washboard or small xylophone make other good percussion instruments. Although you can start by playing along with simple nursery rhyme records which are specially made for children, it's also good to pick out the rhythm from radio music, advertising jingles on TV, etc. It's worth giving time to these games; in early music, rhythm is at least as important as tune.

Costumes

It's important not to be too ambitious when making a costume. Children prefer something simple they can start playing with quickly, rather than something very elaborate that is never quite finished. The more elaborate you make it, the more work you will have to do yourself and the less your child can join in. All these are good reasons for cutting head and arm holes in a simple cardboard box and helping your child to decorate it how he wants to. You may need to stick the objects he chooses on to the box yourself, but let him say what he wants to use to make his costume and why.

Study Box

Different celebrations

Here is a list of a few other celebrations that will help children realize that every country has its special days which everyone, especially children, looks forward to. Your children may well have friends who celebrate some of these days.

Japan Boys' Festival (May 15th). Brightly coloured paper streamers resembling carp (fish noted for energy, power, strength and determination) are tied to poles in the yard or garden to encourage boys to develop similar qualities.
France Fall of the Bastille (July 14th). Fireworks and bonfires celebrate the fall of the main prison in Paris during the French Revolution (1789). Many other festivals around the world make use of fireworks and bonfires.
India Diwali, Festival of Lights (October and November). Candles/oil lamps are lit around balconies and by windows to attract goddess Lakshmi, bringer of fortune and good luck.
USA (and other places) Hallowe'en (October 31st). Children make masks, play games and dress up as witches to drive away evil spirits.

Chinese New Year

Telling a Story

May Ling's New Year

In May Ling's house they had been cleaning and cooking and getting ready for New Year. It was a busy time and everyone worked hard to make the house look nice. What would they need to do? (Tidy, mend, decorate, etc.)

At last, New Year's day came and May Ling's home was soon full of people. Friends came to call and cousins and aunts and uncles shared presents and cakes and wine. There was much laughing and joking. After a while, they all went into the kitchen for the ceremony of the Kitchen God. He was a statue which sat in the kitchen all through the year although May Ling hardly ever noticed him. Her father put honey on his lips and sprinkled him with wine. The Kitchen God didn't seem to notice.

"Why are you doing that, Daddy?" asked May Ling.

"The honey will make him speak sweetly of us and the wine will make him enjoy his journey," replied her father.

"But where is he going?" asked May Ling. "I thought he sat here all through the year."

"At the beginning of each new year, he must go to the Emperor and tell him about our family, how we have behaved and what we have learnt," explained May Ling's dad. "He doesn't go himself, he just sends a message."

"But Daddy, the Emperor doesn't rule us any more," said May Ling.

"No, that's true, and the Kitchen God isn't really going out of the house, but it is very good to remember what we have done in the old year and what we should do in the new year. And it's good to carry on all the old customs from the past so that we can remember that families have done them for years and years. The story of the Kitchen God is a way to remember and to help us all to be wise and kind."

"I don't believe in Kitchen Gods any more," May Ling's dad went on. "All the same, when I walk into the kitchen and see the statue sitting up there, I remember the promises I made at New Year, and I sometimes think he makes the kitchen feel more friendly."

"That's a good idea," said May Ling. "For my New Year promise, I'm going to promise to remember to say good morning to the Kitchen God every day." (Do you think she kept her promise?)

Play and Learn

New Year wishes

Explain that at the Chinese New Year people wish each other a happy New Year and they say, "I hope you have luck, good food, health and a long life and peace". Then ask your child which of those she thinks is most important. What does she say to people on their special days? Ask her to make the best wish she can for someone else. Is there someone in need she might think about?

Paper masks

Masks play an important role in many celebrations and are usually great fun to wear. Large paper bags are most useful. Cut out the eyes and mouth yourself but work with your child to decorate it in any way she wants. Supply pieces of kitchen foil, coloured tissue, leaves from the garden, feathers, bits of egg carton, etc. The mask should be as much fun to make as to wear. Make sure the child can see out of the mask! Excited, but visionless, children can go rushing off in all directions with disastrous results.

Study Box

Chinese horoscopes

The Chinese calendar has a twelve-yearly cycle. Each year is named after an animal which "hides in the heart" of each person born in that year. Here are the dates of the present cycle:

Snake February 18 1977 to February 6 1978	**Boar** February 13 1983 to February 1 1984
Horse February 7 1978 to January 27 1979	**Rat** February 2 1984 to February 19 1985
Sheep January 28 1979 to February 15 1980	**Ox** February 20 1985 to February 8 1986
Monkey February 16 1980 to February 4 1981	**Tiger** February 9 1986 to January 28 1987
Rooster February 5 1981 to January 24 1982	**Rabbit** January 29 1987 to February 16 1988
Dog January 25 1982 to February 12 1983	**Dragon** February 17 1988 to February 5 1989

CELEBRATIONS
International Village

Telling a Story

An international traveller

Sonia's parents worked for the government of their country and their work was to go to other countries and to make friends with people there. Sonia went with them wherever they went even though it meant she had to keep changing school and leaving old friends. She had lived in countries where it was usually hot, countries where it always seemed cold, countries where it hardly ever rained, countries where it seemed to rain all the time. In all those places, Sonia wore different clothes so that she could work and play comfortably whether it was hot, cold, wet or dry.

And Sonia did one special thing to remind her of every country she went to. She collected dolls dressed in the special clothes of each country. Her Japanese doll wore a kimono, her Indian doll a sari, her Nigerian doll wore a George cloth and her Spanish doll wore a mantilla of lace and had a beautiful skirt full of frills and flounces.

Eventually Sonia's family came to live in England. Her new English friends came to visit her and it wasn't long before she took them upstairs to see her dolls. Sonia showed them all her favourites and told them what she remembered most about each country. One of the friends said "Isn't it funny seeing people in such different clothes all the time?" And Sonia burst out laughing.

"People don't wear clothes like that, at least only on special occasions. People really aren't very different at all. Everybody works and plays and eats and sleeps. But I like the different things – it makes life exciting and interesting. And you can choose what you like best from all kinds of different things – clothes, songs, food, games." Do you like anything that comes from another country? Do you know which country it came from?

Play and Learn

International songs

Every now and then, a popular song which can be appreciated all over the world becomes famous. Examples are *Where have all the flowers gone?* and *I'd like to teach the world to sing*. Children easily start humming the tunes of such songs, but it's worth getting them to think of a song everybody knows and asking them why they all like it. Are there big ideas that appeal to most people?

National costumes

Children are bound to want to copy some of the costumes in the picture, and it's a good moment to let them loose in the dressing-up box.

Try to make sure there are some lengths of material for making saris, etc. Some children will simply want to find something that looks as much like a garment in the picture as possible, but others enjoy the creative challenge of adapting a dressing gown or old shirt to a completely new use. Older children may get as far as trying to make special clothes for their dolls, but they will need help to do so. Encourage them to plan what they want and then ask you to finish off for them.

Study Box

International meetings
When international co-operation makes the news on TV, you may find that you can talk generally about activities that bring people from different countries together, even though internationalism is a difficult concept for children to understand.

Sport Many football competitions involve more than two countries. International athletics meetings take place in most years and, of course, the Olympic Games are held once every four years.

Aid All kinds of projects to help countries that are in need or that have suffered a major disaster such as an earthquake are sponsored by the Red Cross, Oxfam and other international agencies.

Politics The United Nations is intended to bring all nations together. Pictures of the politicians in the council chamber give you a chance to talk about people using many different languages, interpreters at work, etc.

Cultural festivals Music and art cross most national barriers and there are usually plenty of chances to point out international artists, musicians, dancers, film stars, etc.

Index

The index contains entries for the Learning Skills, Play and Learn and Study Box sections of this book as well as for the facts and themes discussed with each picture.
Page numbers in *italic* type are references to the Learning Skills and those Study Box sections which aim to help children practise specific skills.
Page numbers in **bold** type are references to the stories and the Play and Learn sections. These include projects, games and other activities which will reinforce the ideas put forward in a particular picture.

Index

The publishers thank the following for their kind co-operation and advice on factual content, and for supplying reference: American Embassy; Children's International Summer Villages; Cyprus High Commission; Hong Kong Tourist Association; Japanese Embassy (Information Centre); New South Wales Government Office; The Scientific Exploration Society (Operation Drake); Swedish Embassy; Swedish National Tourist Office; Trinidad and Tobago Tourist Office.

The publishers thank the teachers and children of the following schools for their help in the preparation of this volume: Maxilla Day Nursery Centre, Notting Hill, London; St James's and St Peter's Primary School, London; Edmund Waller Infants' School, London.

Executive Art Editor	Debra Zuckerman
Editor	Carolyn Ryden
Art Editors	Peter Luff
	Marnie Searchwell
Assistant Text Editor	Edwina Conner
Assistant Art Editor	Mustafa Sami
Researchers	Louis Callan
	Nicholas Law
	Alice Peebles
Assistant Designer	Mary Padden
Project Secretary	Avril Cummings

Four colour origination by Adroit Photo Litho Ltd, Birmingham
Two colour origination by Colourscreens Ltd, Frome
Typesetting by Tradespools Ltd, Frome
Printed in the Netherlands by Koninklijke Smeets Offset B.V.